PRAISE FOR

Generation Friends

"Saul Austerlitz gets at the heart of [the show's] appeal." —*New York*

"[An] under-the-hood chronicle of the nineties sitcom."
—*The New Yorker*

"Austerlitz has written a love letter for fans of the show to remember key moments from the ten-season run of *Friends* while also revealing the good and bad of how difficult it is to create a show, put it on the air, and find lightning in a bottle." —Associated Press

"An engaging read with lots to appeal to *Friends* fans." —*Forbes*

"We might not ever get that reunion special at Central Perk, but Austerlitz has given us the next best thing with this behind-the-scenes look at the world that brought us Monica, Rachel, Ross, Chandler, Phoebe, and Joey." —*Newsweek*

"Saul Austerlitz gives a comprehensive behind-the-scenes look at everyone's favorite show." —*InStyle*

"All die-hard fans need to read this tome, which reveals never-before-known tidbits, including how the show writers' lives inspired the storylines for the beloved characters." —*Star*

"Chock-full of behind-the-scenes info, this fond accounting is a must-read for both new and old *Friends* fans." —*Booklist* (starred review)

"Addictively readable. Come because you're a fan, stay because you realize that *Friends* did (take that, Chandler Bing!) define a cultural moment: a world where coffee shops were just beginning to take off as 'third places,' television wasn't available to DVR or stream, and networks were starting to warm up to sitcoms about nothing. I'm halfway through Saul Austerlitz's ode to this NBC hit, and I can't wait to finish it and annoy my friends with fun *Friends* facts."

—Sarah Gelman,
director of books and editorial for the Amazon Book Review blog

"A treat for *Friends* fans, from OG must-see-TV viewers to the new generation of streamers, full of insights into what made a quintessential '90s phenomenon into a lasting, international classic for the ages. You'll get your share of juicy behind-the-scenes tidbits, from vicious writers'-room debates about Rachel and Joey's romance to the time the producers almost moved the setting to Minneapolis (seriously). But you'll also get a hit of nostalgia for a time when an entire nation hung on the fate of Ross and Rachel, and plenty of smart analysis of why *Friends* was the right show at the right time . . . and also continues to be the right show at an entirely different time."

—Jennifer Keishin Armstrong,
New York Times bestselling author of *Seinfeldia*

"*Friends* wasn't just a funny show—it was a generational work of art that evolved television's scope. It proved that shows could travel beyond the dynamics of nuclear families and the virtue of strong cast chemistry. In *Generation Friends*, Saul Austerlitz transports us back to Central Perk with our eternal friends trying to find their place in the world. Just as importantly, he lifts the curtain to provide a sprawling behind-the-scenes look at its creation, enactment, and still-growing legacy."

—Jonathan Abrams,
New York Times bestselling author of *All the Pieces Matter*

"With careful research and new and revealing interviews, Austerlitz's *Generation Friends* does what a great behind-the-scenes book should do: It'll make you want to rewatch the entire series again from start to finish, with a new appreciation of everything from the writing and acting to set design and costumes. Better yet, Austerlitz provides some much-needed validation for those of us who never warmed to the whole Ross-Rachel thing, assuring us that we *might* have been on to something, even as he argues we were wrong. FIGHT ME, SAUL."

—Brian Jay Jones,
New York Times bestselling author of *Jim Henson: The Biography* and *Becoming Dr. Seuss*

"The ultimate peek behind the scenes into the creation and execution of the series that broke new ground with its inclusion of a lesbian wedding and other LGBTQ-related storylines." —*Baltimore Outloud*

"On its twenty-fifth anniversary, the show's die-hard fans will love Austerlitz's detailed, discerning, and sumptuous history." —*Kirkus Reviews*

"Guiding readers through Hollywood politics, notes from the network, and a complicated casting process, the author documents the creation of the legendary television show. . . . Austerlitz also goes behind the scenes, detailing overnight writing sessions, contract negotiations, and disagreements with directors. . . . For followers of the program and lovers of pop culture." —*Library Journal*

ALSO BY SAUL AUSTERLITZ

Just a Shot Away:
Peace, Love, and Tragedy with the Rolling Stones at Altamont

Sitcom:
A History in 24 Episodes from I Love Lucy *to* Community

Another Fine Mess:
A History of American Film Comedy

Money for Nothing:
A History of the Music Video from the Beatles to the White Stripes

GENERATION FRIENDS

**An Inside Look at the Show
That Defined a Television Era**

SAUL AUSTERLITZ

DUTTON

DUTTON
An imprint of Penguin Random House LLC
penguinrandomhouse.com

Previously published in a Dutton hardcover edition in September 2019

First Dutton trade paperback edition: September 2020

Credit information for photo insert:
Photos 1–10: Getty Images
Photos 11–20: Copyright © Bruza Brother Productions, LLC

THE LIBRARY OF CONGRESS HAS CATALOGUED THE HARDCOVER EDITION AS FOLLOWS:

Names: Austerlitz, Saul, author.
Title: Generation Friends : an inside look at the show that defined a television era / Saul Austerlitz.
Description: New York, NY : Dutton, an imprint of Penguin Random House [2019] | Includes bibliographical references.
Identifiers: LCCN 2018058454 (print) | LCCN 2019013605 (ebook) | ISBN 9781524743376 (ebook) | ISBN 9781524743352 (hc)
Subjects: LCSH: Friends (Television program)
Classification: LCC PN1992.77.F76 (ebook) | LCC PN1992.77.F76 A97 2019 (print) | DDC 791.45/72—dc23
LC record available at https://lccn.loc.gov/2018058454

Dutton trade paperback ISBN: 9781524743369

Printed in the United States of America
10 9 8 7 6 5 4 3 2 1

BOOK DESIGN BY KRISTIN DEL ROSARIO

For Nate,
my favorite new reader

CONTENTS

GENERATION FRIENDS

INTRODUCTION

They would gather, every few minutes, in clumps and packs. They were wielding smartphones, of course, and digital cameras, and disposable models you might pick up at a souvenir shop or pharmacy checkout counter. There were mothers posing with their daughters, European couples who looked as if they had only just stepped off the runway in Milan, and amateur photographers setting up shoots in the middle of the street.

My friend Jennifer and I were having lunch, and we both found ourselves distracted by the onslaught of humanity in the street, although of course we were there for much the same reasons. We were at the Little Owl, a twenty-eight-seat restaurant in the West Village that describes itself as "a corner gem with a big porkchop and an even bigger heart." We were there for the superb food, but more so for the location. Based on the establishing shot that displayed the building's exterior, the Little Owl was in the spot where Central Perk would have been—you know, if it ever existed. We were on a brief tour to find the traces of *Friends* in the real New York of early 2018, and we were beginning our search with the polenta (for Jennifer) and the eggplant parmigiana (for me).

There was something ludicrous and obsessive about our expedition. *Friends* had not only been filmed on a soundstage on the Warner Bros. lot in Los Angeles, it had contained only the faintest traces of New York, regardless of its claims to residency. We were equipped with a blog post listing some of the purported locations of the characters' apartments and a handful of other West Village destinations that the show explicitly mentioned or featured as an exterior. The list, which included Ross's apartment, Phoebe's apartment, and the Lucille Lortel Theatre, where Joey had performed in a show, was short.

Friends lacked even the New York credibility of *Sex and the City* or *Seinfeld,* two other comedy series of the era that had used the city as a backdrop. They had at least made New York a kind of permanent supporting character on their shows, whereas *Friends,* after a few brief forays onto the subway or into Bloomingdale's, had retreated into its preferred interior spaces, including the faux neighborhood spot whose spiritual footprint we were now occupying.

Throughout our lunch, we anticipated the arrival of fellow *Friends* fanatics, there to commune with the setting of their favorite show. But no one even approached the restaurant. They were mostly standing catty-corner to the restaurant, on the northwest side of the street. The collective agreement to stand only on that corner was baffling. Why not get a bit closer?

Once Jennifer and I concluded our meal and stepped outside ourselves, the riddle answered itself almost instantaneously. Standing on the northwest corner, of course, placed the façade of the familiar building at 90 Bedford Street directly in the backdrop of fans' selfies, looking just as it had on television. After all, 90 Bedford had only ever been glimpsed in brief establishing shots on *Friends,* and only ever from a single angle. To photograph it from any other perspective would be to render it entirely unrecognizable. This was the perspective they wanted to see, and share, and post.

To be a *Friends* fan touring the West Village in search of relics from the show was to grasp at any and all straws. Ross's apartment was supposed to be across the street, but while we had the address, the building did not look much like it had on the show—or perhaps we were remembering it wrong. And the same went for 90 Bedford. Seeing the building—even eating lunch inside it—the mind balked at the notion that Rachel and Monica and Chandler and Joey were supposed to have lived right here. Real and imaginary geography did not line up, and it was next to impossible to picture this twenty-first-century bistro superimposed atop that orange couch, and Gunther hunched behind the counter.

There was so little to see on our *Friends* walking tour that after checking in on Ross, we walked five minutes to 5 Morton Street, where Phoebe was supposed to live, and wound up our corkscrew-shaped tour at the Lucille Lortel Theatre, where Joey had once performed. While I suppose we could have stopped in at Bloomingdale's, where Rachel had worked, or the Plaza, where Monica and Chandler had celebrated their engagement, how much would it have added to our understanding of *Friends'* place in New York?

The tour felt like a letdown, even though I had known there was practically nothing to see, but I kept thinking about those tourists who had ventured to the corner of Grove and Bedford to pay homage to the show they loved. There was essentially nothing to do other than snap a selfie, but they kept coming, from New Jersey and from Europe and from everywhere else *Friends* pilgrims originated. The lack of anything worth seeing was not a marker of their being hoodwinked; it demonstrated the ferocity of their devotion that they were there nonetheless, present in the West Village to see nothing much at all simply because it had been granted the mark of *Friends*.

In coming to visit *Friends* places, it was hard not to ponder the remarkable life and afterlife of this show, which seemingly reached new heights of the impossibly mundane upon its premiere in 1994 and yet still captivates new audiences a quarter of a century later. There was so little to look at, at first glance, and yet it was impossible to look away. *Friends* had emerged in an era when comedies were finding new ways to amuse their audiences by being about as little as possible. At the same time, *Friends*' comic minimalism was conjoined to a soap-operatic maximalism. It was a show that compelled us to stay glued to our screens by the promise of emotional revelation. Its characters, often so devoid of ambition or drive, were rendered whole by the force of their yearning: for romance, for sex, for understanding. There were teenagers around the United States—around the world, for that matter—who discovered *Friends* and believed it to be their own. As someone who had been a teenager himself when the show premiered, I was fascinated by that desire to claim the show as theirs. Television was almost inevitably a cultural product with an expiration date attached. How often did viewers go back and watch series that had premiered decades prior, unless out of nostalgic drift?

I wanted to tell the story of a show that had been created in an entirely different media universe—before streaming, before #MeToo, before the War on Terror, before Trump—and understand the roots of its success. By delving into the particulars of the making of the show, I hoped to understand how *Friends* had achieved its remarkable success, and how it had sustained that appeal across decades, and generations of viewers.

Friends' perceived weaknesses had become its strengths. Its lack of realism (Chandler and Joey living in the West Village?) had been transformed, through the passage of time, into an evergreen fantasy of youth. It was a show about young people that would be discovered, year after year, by new cohorts of young people aching to know what adulthood would be like. The show may not have had much of anything to do with New York, but people continued to come to New York to see what they could of the show they loved so fiercely. They were here to say thank you.

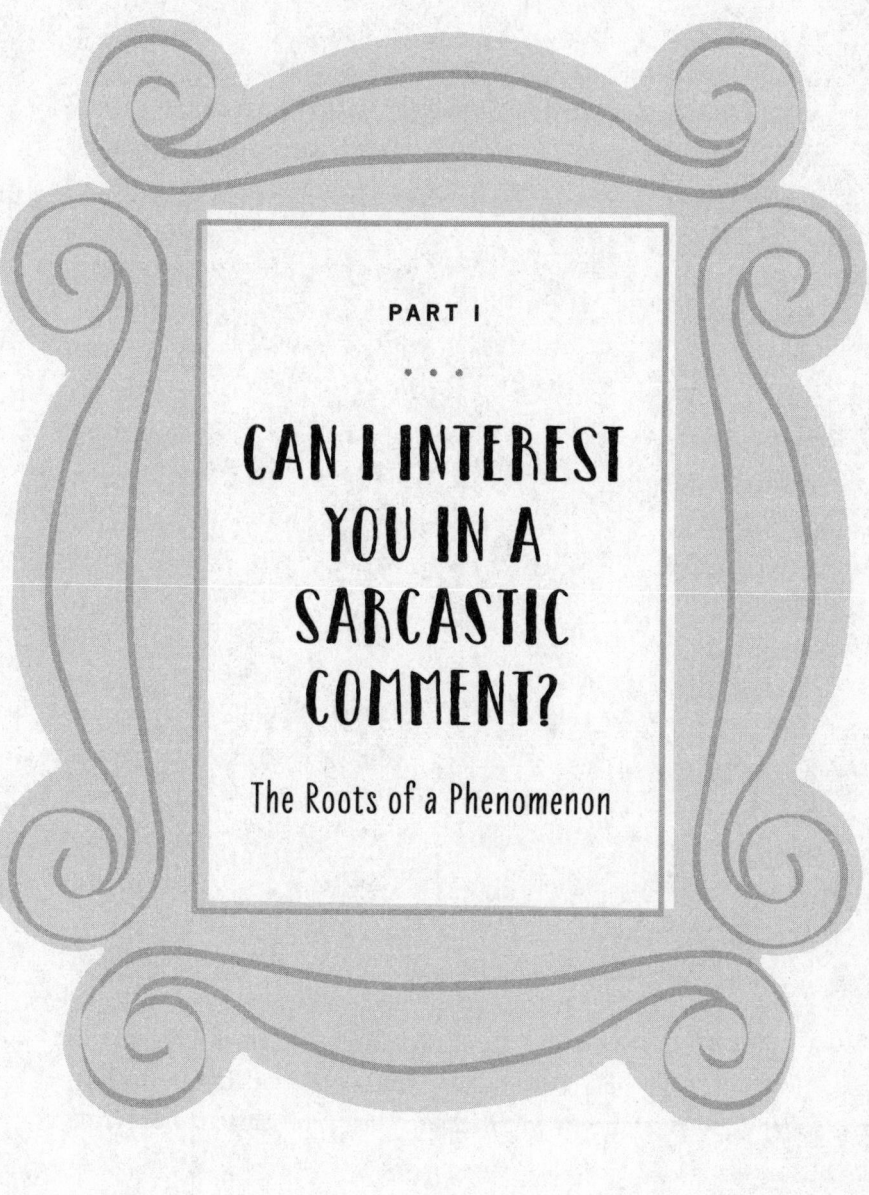

PART I

. . .

CAN I INTEREST YOU IN A SARCASTIC COMMENT?

The Roots of a Phenomenon

CHAPTER 1

INSOMNIA CAFÉ

A TV Show Is Born

One day in late 1993, a young television writer named Marta Kauffman was driving along Beverly Boulevard when she passed a funky coffee shop called Insomnia Café, located across the street from an Orthodox synagogue. Full of lumpy couches and garish chairs, strings of Christmas lights, and towering bookshelves piled high with mismatched books, the place was a beacon calling to the artists and slackers of the Fairfax–La Brea area. Kauffman, who lived nearby in Hancock Park, was trawling for ideas that could be transformed into stories for the upcoming pilot season.

Along with her writing partner David Crane, Kauffman had created the groundbreaking HBO series *Dream On* and, after leaving the show, had been fruitlessly seeking network success. Last pilot season had been disappointing, and it was important to the two writers that 1994 be a better year for them than 1993 had been. Something about Insomnia Café grabbed her attention, and she began to mull over an intriguing idea. Could a comedy series set in a coffee shop appeal to viewers? Kauffman and Crane had only recently moved to California from New York, and found that they missed their old crew of friends from Manhattan terribly. They had spent all their spare time together, done everything together, served as a kind of surrogate family. What if they put together a show about that?

———

Sometime in the mid-1980s, Warren Littlefield discovered something new about television. The NBC executive, protégé to network president Brandon Tartikoff, was attending an advertising meeting, and the research department displayed a gridded chart showing the relative audience shares for two shows: CBS's *Murder, She Wrote* and NBC's own *St. Elsewhere*. At the bottom left, *Murder, She Wrote*, featuring Angela Lansbury as a crime-solving mystery novelist, a fixture in the Nielsen top ten, and at the top right, NBC's quirky hospital drama, beloved by critics but lagging noticeably in the ratings. The message was clear: NBC's niche effort was having its clock cleaned. What came next changed Littlefield's entire career.

If you think *Murder, She Wrote* is kicking *St. Elsewhere*'s ass, the researcher continued, you're right—when it comes to total audience. Now a new graph replaced the initial chart. This one showed the fees networks charged advertisers for their shows. Quirky, niche, never-gonna-be-a-hit *St. Elsewhere* made NBC more money than the far more successful *Murder, She Wrote* made for CBS. NBC was able to charge more for its thirty-second spots than CBS charged for theirs.

And why? The answer lay in a steady shift in advertisers' interests. Advertisers increasingly preferred younger eyeballs. Reaching a mass audience was too diffuse and too unpredictable. Advertisers preferred a targeted approach, pushing their sports cars and light beers to youthful viewers, whom they believed to be more likely to purchase them. The ratings were no less important today than they had been yesterday, but the youth market—broadly speaking, viewers between the ages of eighteen and forty-nine—was becoming the only market that really mattered. (Older people, the thinking went, could be safely ignored, being unlikely to buy the razors and sports cars and beer advertisers hoped to sell.) Littlefield understood that the ground was shifting in network television.

Littlefield had been studying government at American University in Washington, DC, during the final years of Richard Nixon's presidency, imagining himself rescuing American democracy from unconstitutional knavery. When Nixon resigned, the urgency of Littlefield's cause dissipated, and he switched to studying psychology. Before beginning a graduate program, he wanted to accrue some work experience and was offered a job by a hometown friend as a gofer at a production company.

After stints as a location scout and an assistant editor, Littlefield was acquiring properties of his own for production. He was feeding original movies to the gaping maw of the networks, which had approximately three hundred such slots to fill on their yearly calendars. One such effort, an East Africa–set adventure called *The Last Giraffe,* was selected by *The Hollywood Reporter* as one of the ten best TV movies of 1979, and Littlefield decided it was time to relocate to Los Angeles. He soon took up a job at NBC in comedy development and began his meteoric rise at the network.

Just a few years after the *St. Elsewhere* epiphany, Littlefield was named the president of entertainment at NBC, replacing Tartikoff. Littlefield was inheriting a network that was simultaneously flourishing and endangered. Under the tutelage of the highly esteemed Tartikoff, NBC had dominated the 1980s with series like *Cheers, The Cosby Show,* and *L.A. Law.* Tartikoff had been skeptical about a new series from two comedians named Jerry Seinfeld and Larry David ("too New York and too Jewish," said the New York Jew) but developed the acerbic, highconcept, defiantly unlikable *Seinfeld* anyway.

Now Littlefield had succeeded Tartikoff and was watching as the network's most beloved series were leaving the air. *The Cosby Show* had ended, *Cheers* was ending, and NBC's historic run of dominance on Thursday nights was running the risk of coming to an end. NBC needed to develop some new shows, and Littlefield's newfound fixation on younger audiences found him constructing a mental graph of his own. The x-axis was the mass market; the y-axis was the youth audience. Littlefield was aiming to simultaneously maximize both, creating shows that were appealing to younger viewers without turning away older audiences.

As Littlefield was pondering his future audience, Bill Clinton was close to wrapping up his first year as president and soon to face a wipeout in the 1994 midterms, in which Republicans would gain fifty-four seats and make Newt Gingrich Speaker of the House. The Soviet Union had collapsed two years prior, leaving the United States as the sole world superpower. Democracy had seemingly won its titanic struggle with world communism without firing a shot. The American way of life was ascendant.

The sports world was about to be rocked by the news that, for the first time in ninety years, there would be no World Series played that fall, due to a labor strike. Quentin Tarantino won the Palme d'Or at Cannes for his neo-Godardian crime film *Pulp Fiction*, which resuscitated the moribund career of John Travolta, and the dominant film of the summer would be the overpraised, conservative *Forrest Gump*, in which Tom Hanks's title character was present at much of postwar American history while serving as proof that all was as it should be. Independent film was ascendant, with Miramax, run by the later-to-be-disgraced Harvey Weinstein, leading a phalanx of new voices with films like *The Crying Game*. In the mid-1990s, film was still considered the primary visual medium of the American arts, attracting exciting new voices like Tarantino, Todd Haynes, John Singleton, and Allison Anders. Television, by comparison, while it had produced exciting new series like *Seinfeld* and *NYPD Blue*, was considered a backwater, a place you went when the movies didn't work out, whose audience was far less discerning than film's.

Meanwhile, a coffee company that had originally been started by two teachers and a writer in Seattle had begun to expand beyond the

Pacific Northwest. Starbucks had opened stores in Portland and Chicago, and then targeted California, tackling San Francisco and Los Angeles. The company had gone from eleven stores in 1987 to one hundred sixty-one stores only five years later. Coffee was suddenly big business, and Starbucks was rapidly becoming the name most prominently associated with coffeehouse culture. With its oversize plush chairs, its soothing soundtrack of folk, indie rock, and world music, and its distinct language (who decided that a "tall" would be one of the smaller sizes for its drinks?), what had once been associated with college campuses and Greenwich Village was soon to be a nationwide phenomenon. Coffee was no longer solely a matter of dumping hot water into powder over the kitchen sink; it was now an entire lifestyle, with a culture of (occasionally harried) leisure to accompany it. Young Americans would not just drink coffee for a burst of caffeine; they would lounge around in coffeehouses, bantering, laughing, and trading confidences, seizing on the relatively new spaces forming in cities across the nation and making them their own.

As president, Littlefield was carrying with him the message he had received from the legendary former NBC CEO and chairman Grant Tinker earlier in his career. Tinker had continually sought to remind Littlefield and his colleagues that the audience was not an alien race. What shows were his employees breathlessly anticipating each week? What series would convince them to cancel their plans and rush home, in this pre-streaming era, to catch the latest episode? Those were the shows they should be making. It was time for stories that spoke to the audiences they craved, that were about young people.

And if the story of the sitcom could be said to have followed an arc, one of the major changes that had unfolded across the four decades of television history had been the shift away from the family show. Television had begun as a domestic medium, a place for families to gather in their living rooms to watch other, fictional families in their living rooms. It had been a feminine counterpoint to the increasingly masculine sphere of the movies. But over time, the domestic families of *Father Knows Best* and *Leave It to Beaver* had given way to the workplace families of *The Mary Tyler Moore Show* and *M*A*S*H*.

With the American family dissolving and re-forming in unimaginable new patterns, the sitcom increasingly preferred its groupings of colleagues and squads. The 1980s had seen a resurgence of the family sitcom, with the former B-movie-star-turned-national-father-figure Ronald Reagan inspiring a wave of sturdy sitcom dads like *The Cosby Show*'s Heathcliff Huxtable and *Family Ties*' Steven Keaton. Ratings indicated that younger audiences, less likely to be married or raising children, mostly preferred to see themselves reflected on their television screens, and even older, married viewers were often happier watching a crew of friends bantering.

Seinfeld was a show like that. The specials department at NBC, not the prime-time programming team, had picked up the pilot in 1989. Rick Ludwin and his group had fallen in love with a stand-up comedian named Jerry Seinfeld. Seinfeld and fellow comedian Larry David had spent an afternoon walking around a Manhattan deli and talking about the strange products on display there, belatedly realizing that their aimless banter could form the foundation of a new kind of television series. The pilot flopped with audiences, and NBC expressed little enthusiasm for the show, but Ludwin's fierce advocacy bankrolled a four-episode run, and eventually got it an invitation for a fuller second season.

Seinfeld rewrote the rules of the sitcom. Its characters were amoral, callous, and self-centered. There were no meaningful romantic relationships on the show; the one partnership heading toward marriage would later be brutally, hilariously interrupted by a batch of poisoned envelopes. And yet, NBC understood that part of the attraction of *Seinfeld* was its aura of charming Manhattan singles in pursuit of true love—or at least a fruitful one-night stand. Much of *Seinfeld* was turned over to the logistics and limitations of big-city dating, with many of its most memorable moments, from "They're real, and they're spectacular" to

"Not that there's anything wrong with that," stemming from relationship stories. People enjoyed watching George and Elaine and Kramer sitting on Jerry's couch and bantering, and NBC was betting that there was a huge untapped market for series similar to *Seinfeld*, the third-highest-rated series of the 1993–94 season after *60 Minutes* and *Home Improvement*. The search for the next *Seinfeld* was on.

Each morning at six o'clock, Littlefield received a fax from the research department, based in New York, with the overnight ratings. It was like a daily report card, delivering updated assessments of the audience's feelings regarding NBC programming. As Littlefield perused the overnights from San Francisco and Houston and Atlanta, he thought about what it must be like to be a young person starting a life in one of those places. Rent was expensive, jobs were scarce, and moving somewhere new, beyond the reach of parents and old friends, could be lonely. Littlefield considered his own formative postcollege years, living with roommates in the suburbs of New York and taking the commuter train to work daily. It had been harsh and unromantic, but it had also been a testing ground. To be young was to scuffle, but it was also to discover the world afresh. ABC was flying high with blue-collar comedies like *Roseanne* and *Home Improvement*, and CBS was devoted to its older audience, seemingly unaware of the advertising pot of gold that Littlefield was chasing. No one was serving the younger viewers Littlefield had in mind.

Littlefield put out a call to writers and producers he had worked with: Bring me ideas for shows about young people. He was in search of stories about breaking away, about stepping out, about finding yourself. Littlefield was convinced that older audiences could easily be compelled to watch a show in which they communed with their younger selves, but younger audiences could never be cajoled to watch characters living lives they had not yet experienced. Littlefield didn't want any more pitches about crusading lawyers or wholesome single dads; he wanted clever, warmhearted shows with instantly recognizable characters. He wanted a kinder, gentler *Seinfeld*—less New York and less Jewish (while maybe still retaining some of the original's Semitic, five-boroughs appeal). He didn't get it.

The first batch of pitch meetings came and went, and a few scripts were given the green light for development, but nothing of substance propelled itself forward. None of them felt unique, and Littlefield went about his business, conscious that there was an opportunity that might vanish. Another network might grab the reins, and NBC's chance to win over a new generation of viewers, and the resulting advertising dollars, might dissipate.

For television writers, pilot season, the weeks when writers proposed new concepts for television series to the networks bidding for their services, was a hectic flurry of all-night writing sessions and snap decisions that even the people involved could hardly remember. To maximize one's options, it was customary for working writers to pitch two, or even three, pilots to networks, in the hopes that one might catch fire. Marta Kauffman and David Crane were hoping to expunge the bad taste that still lingered in their mouths from the preceding season.

Jeff Sagansky at CBS had been happy to listen to Crane and Kauffman's pitches during the 1993 pilot season, including an idea for a musical show with original songs each week, but had his own ideas. He was looking for a white-collar version of the bickering, loving family of *Roseanne*, he told them, and was not much interested in anything else. Kauffman and Crane came back with *Family Album*, which was meant to fulfill Sagansky's desire.

Crane believed that some shows fed you exciting angles, new story lines, and rich characters, and some simply didn't. *Family Album*, about a California doctor (played by Peter Scolari) who moves to Philadelphia along with his family to look after his parents, didn't. After six episodes, CBS canceled the show. Kauffman and Crane concentrated their efforts on the next pilot season.

Kauffman and Crane had cocreated the critically admired HBO comedy series *Dream On* (1990–96), in which Brian Benben's randy divorced book editor ran through a seemingly infinite array of beautiful young women interested in bedding him. Benben's Martin, raised by television, finds his endless romantic snafus punctuated in his mind by clips from old movies and TV shows, offering a stream of witty and arch commentary on the show's plotlines.

Dream On was a superb opportunity for Kauffman and Crane, but they were surprised to discover how exhausting it could be to produce a show with only one star. Benben was a fine actor, but given that he had to appear in almost every scene, production could become a slog. If Benben was tired or under the weather, the show would have to halt until he recovered. It was simply too much pressure to place on one performer. The next time they had an opportunity to put a show on the air, Kauffman and Crane promised themselves, they would work with an ensemble.

The failure of *Family Album* had dinged their reputation some, which meant that the next show had to be fresher—had to be something that emerged from their own hearts and memories. For the 1994 pilot season, Kauffman and Crane hammered out three new ideas. *Dream On* had made them a sought-after commodity at the networks, who were looking for something equally creative, if less sexually explicit. They talked it over with Warner Bros. Television president Leslie Moonves and the other Warner Bros. executives and settled on a plan, based on the four networks' open time slots for the fall and their rough preferences regarding what kinds of shows, and audiences, they were in search of. At the time, there were only four broadcast networks producing original programming, and independent production companies like Warner Bros. would create shows that they might sell to any of the networks.

They would begin with their idea for a show about high schoolers who express their feelings by bursting into song, a kind of *Glee* two decades before Ryan Murphy's show. ABC had told them that they wanted their own *Dream On*, but when they came back with the idea for a single-camera comedy, the network was disappointed. They wanted to know where the laugh track was. *Dream On* had no laugh track, either, but it was rapidly evident that ABC was not ready yet for single-camera comedies like *The Larry Sanders Show*, which was generally considered to be for more sophisticated audiences than the traditional three-camera sitcom setup still prevalent on network TV. ABC passed on the high school show—"As soon as a couple of words left our mouths, their eyes glazed over," Kauffman would tell a reporter—but the other two moved forward. Networks paid lip service to the idea of breaking the rules, but more often than not, they preferred the rules to the chaos of the new.

Fox took the next step and ordered a script for their show *Reality Check*, a single-camera series about a teenage boy with a vivid imagination. The idea was that, as with *Dream On*, audiences would be afforded glimpses into the mind of its protagonist—first called Harry, then later renamed Jamie. And there was still one more idea to hash out, a comedy series about twentysomethings that they believed might be a good fit for youth-oriented Fox as well.

They had come up with the idea while sitting at their desks in their Warner Bros. office, surrounded by posters from their New York theatrical productions, taking up a pose similar to the ones they had struck in other rooms for the last decade and a half. Kauffman and Crane had met as sophomores at Brandeis University when they were both cast in a production of Tennessee Williams's *Camino Real*. Kauffman played a prostitute, and Crane was a street waif.

When he was growing up, Crane was sure he was going to be an actor. He would watch his favorite television shows, smart, character-based series like *The Mary Tyler Moore Show*, and daydream about what a career as a performer might be like. Crane imagined a life in the arts, and being an actor seemed like the most straightforward route to success. When he arrived at Brandeis University, Crane dove into the school's theater scene, and it took a number of years before he came to a realization: He was not, and would never be, much of an actor.

After *Camino Real*, Kauffman was asked to direct a production of Stephen Schwartz and John-Michael Tebelak's *Godspell* at school and approached Crane about casting him in the show. Crane turned down the part but offered to codirect, and a partnership was formed. They bonded over their mutual affection for *The Dick Van Dyke Show* and its miniaturist plots. The presence of Rose Marie as a member of the show-within-the-show's writing staff had demonstrated to Kauffman that women could be television writers, even if Kauffman felt like Rose Marie's character, Sally Rogers, was around mostly to order sandwiches for the other writers.

Kauffman had been an aspiring actor and writer as an adolescent when an AP English teacher told her that she was the least perceptive student he had ever had. She would, in case she bore any illusions to the contrary, never be a writer. The high school senior accepted her teacher's harsh verdict and began her time at Brandeis University primarily interested in acting. It took some time for the sting of her teacher's comments to wear off enough for her to realize that she enjoyed writing substantially more than acting. What's more, she was good at it.

Kauffman and Crane branched out from directing to writing their own original material. Their show *Personals*, a musical about characters who place personal ads, was well received at Brandeis. After graduation, Kauffman and Crane moved to New York and began writing shows of their own in earnest, along with Seth Friedman. Kauffman and Crane contributed songs and poetry for the musical *A . . . My Name Is Alice* (1984), a revue conceived and directed by Joan Micklin Silver and Julianne Boyd. *Alice* was a compendium of songs about women, with Kauffman and Crane contributing a song called "Trash"—although, notably, not the number called "Friends." *Personals* received an off-Broadway run in 1985, with Kauffman's husband, Michael Skloff (who had once been Crane's roommate), serving as musical director and composing some additional material for the show.

Alice's success—*New York Times* theater critic Frank Rich called it "delightful"—attracted the attention of an agent, ICM's Nancy

Josephson, whom they signed on with. They worked on a series of shows for TheaterWorksUSA, which commissioned musical theater for inner-city children, and then were approached by the rights holders to the Dudley Moore film *Arthur*. Kauffman, Crane, and Skloff were hired to put together a musical version of *Arthur*, which occupied the next five years of their careers before stalling.

After Crane and Kauffman had been working in New York theater for about five years, a young television agent came to the theater one night to attend their latest show. She approached the partners after the show and asked them if they had ever thought about writing for television. Neither had, but the agent strongly encouraged them to give it a try.

Most writers looking to transition to television would move to Los Angeles and look for a staff-writer job on a show, but Crane and Kauffman wound up taking an unexpected route. Neither was ready to leave New York, or the theater, so the agent recommended that they come up with ten ideas for new shows. She would take them and shop them around, and see if she could drum up any interest in them.

Crane and Kauffman painstakingly came up with the requested ideas and began flying out occasionally to Los Angeles to pitch them in person. Theater was engrossing and emotionally rewarding, but when the two writers turned thirty with little financial success to show for their efforts, California beckoned. They took a job in development for Norman Lear's production company. They were in the television industry but still were not in a writers' room, where they would have been working on someone else's show, fleshing out someone else's ideas, and serving someone else's concepts. Consciously or not, Crane and Kauffman were intent on protecting their voices from the incursion of other influences.

On *Dream On*, which had developed out of a desire to utilize the rights to Universal's film library, Crane ran the writers' room with Kauffman, who also oversaw the onstage work, and Kevin Bright, who had become their partner, took charge of postproduction. Each of the three partners had their own discrete but overlapping role, allowing them control of a single aspect of television production while also ensuring that the others were aware of, and included in, their work.

***

For as long as he could remember, Kevin Bright had known he did not want to be in show business. His father, Jackie, had started off as a vaudeville comic and then transitioned into work as a personal manager for Catskills acts. He would book comedians and other performers for breakfast and brunch acts, or to appear on cruise ships. Jackie would bring Kevin to the Concord Resort Hotel, part of the legendary Borscht Belt. Bright's family had photographs of him as an exhausted little boy asleep in the lap of none other than Sammy Davis Jr.

Kevin knew he was not cut out for the life of the showbiz hustler. By the time he enrolled in college, he had decided to study philosophy, which was about as far away as you could get from the Catskills. After he enrolled in an elective film course, he realized philosophy was not in the cards for him. Entertainment had possibilities that were tremendously appealing to him. Bright transferred to Emerson College in Boston, which had a highly regarded film-and-television program, and decided to immerse himself in the very thing he had always thought was not for him.

Bright had been raised in the fading light of vaudeville and was passionate about its television inheritor, the variety show—the place where his childhood experience met his passion for the moving image. When he graduated, he went to work for producer Joseph Cates, whose brother Gilbert would eventually produce the annual Academy Awards telecast. Bright began by fetching coffee, and by the end of his six-year run with Cates, he was producing variety specials of his own. He produced five David Copperfield specials, the Miss Teenage America pageant, and a number of Johnny Cash specials in the late 1970s and 1980s. Bright had practically cornered the market on variety television produced in New

York, but in doing so, he realized that the business was dying. There were fewer and fewer specials being made, and those that remained were being made in California.

Bright decided to make the leap to Los Angeles, and to comedy. Bright's history in variety had granted him an accidental specialty in maximizing minimalist budgets. HBO was looking to get away with making half-hour comedy programming in the low six figures, and Bright knew how to do it. He went on to produce comic specials for Paul Shaffer, Harry Shearer, and Merrill Markoe. Bright would also produce the first original-to-syndication sitcom, sold directly to local stations instead of to a network, *Madame's Place* (1982), shooting seventy-five episodes of the adventures of a faded-movie-star puppet named Madame in just eighteen weeks.

Bright had been brought in for *Dream On* by noted director John Landis (*The Blues Brothers, Animal House*). Landis was looking to branch out into television but needed an experienced hand to walk him through the work of packaging and producing for TV. Landis had been offered the opportunity to make use of Universal's remarkable film archive and was in search of marketable ideas when he was introduced to Kauffman and Crane. Bright had not worked in six months when, all at once, he was hired for *Dream On* and for the pilot of *In Living Color*, a new comedy sketch series for Fox. It was Bright, a music buff, who convinced Damon Wayans and David Alan Grier to use the Weather Girls' "It's Raining Men" for the sketch featuring their flamboyantly gay film critics, "Men on Film." Bright assumed that he would stay on with *In Living Color*, a network show, but when that opportunity fell through for him, he happily became a producer on *Dream On*.

After a number of years of working together on *Dream On*, Kauffman, Bright, and Crane were sitting around their office one day when Kauffman wanted to share her enthusiasm over their professional arrangement, with she and Crane serving as writers and Bright producing. "This is so great," she told Bright and Crane. "Wouldn't it be great if we could just keep doing this?" "We could, if you want to," Bright told her, and beginning in 1993, the three partners had an overall deal with Warner Bros. to produce new television series. That year had not been their year, but now it was 1994, and Kevin Bright was free to throw himself into finding a spot in the network lineup for the fall.

———

Fox immediately began bombarding Kauffman and Crane with suggested changes to *Reality Check,* the show that brought viewers inside the mind of a teenager. The network desperately wanted the show to be raunchier than it was, more like a Fox-friendly *Dream On.* Couldn't Harry (or Jamie) be older? Couldn't he already be driving? Couldn't he be having sex? Their protagonist did indeed become older, a high school junior, not a freshman, and the bulging script was trimmed down by losing some characters, including his father.

Reality Check was another headache, just like *Family Album* had been. The network wanted something new, but then wanted that new thing to be as familiar as possible. Kauffman and Crane knew they had made their name with a high-concept series, but Crane in particular was drawn to the idea of an ultra-low-concept show. Sitting in their office on the Warner Bros. lot, Kauffman and Crane began to banter about their own group of friends from New York, a sextet that also included a lesbian couple. They borrowed personality traits from acquaintances and from actors they had worked with, melding together a hodgepodge of characteristics into loose outlines for their protagonists. In the evenings, Kauffman pulled aside two of the babysitters who helped care for her children to quiz them about life as a single twentysomething.

The two writers drafted a seven-page pitch document to be shared with networks, detailing the characters, the setting, and some of the adventures they imagined unfolding. "It's about searching for love and commitment and security . . . and a fear of love and commitment and security," they wrote. "And it's about friendship, because when you're young and single in the city, your friends are your family."

"That's basically it," they closed the pitch document. "And even if we are going to play with the form a little bit, ultimately, it's about six people who you can invest in. For us, it's kind of like writing six Martin Tuppers."

There were bits of the creators themselves in their characters. Kauffman put more than a touch of herself into the character of Monica, whom she thought of as being someone who always needed to close the marker until it clicked. Monica was worn out by an endless schedule of dating. "She feels like if she has to eat another Caesar salad, she's going to die," Kauffman told a *New York Times* reporter chronicling that year's pilot season.

Traces of Crane could be found in the dry, acerbic wit of Chandler. Crane, who is gay, initially thought of making Chandler's character gay as well, which would have notably changed the story arc of the series to come. Chandler wound up straight, but the kind of straight man Crane envisioned getting regularly mistaken for gay. (A college friend of Kauffman's named Chandler would later jokingly accuse her of having ruined his life by giving a *Friends* character his name.) Kauffman also saw some of herself in the antic spirituality of Phoebe.

The truth was, though, there simply was not enough time to put too much thought into these characters. "WRITE FASTER," they urged themselves via a message scribbled on their blackboard as the deadline for the script neared. Then the message subtly changed: "WRITE BETTER."

The two writers, then in their midthirties, kept it simple. They would pitch the series as being about six intertwined characters, in and out of one another's apartments and one another's lives as they went about the ordinary business of their daily existence. Crucially, they wanted a story with three female protagonists who were given equal time and equal heft. They were not just girlfriends, or sisters, or funny sidekicks. Kauffman would later insist that no script ever contain the word *bitch* (or, for that matter, the phrase *shut up*). Kauffman and Crane even came up with a tagline they would present to the networks they pitched to: "It's that time of life when your friends are your family."

Crane was more than satisfied with their minimal work. If they had the six characters they were looking for and the setting was roughly acceptable, it was good enough to pitch. To be a television writer was to endlessly spin out new characters, new situations, new juicy story lines. These were just the latest iteration from two hamsters trapped on the Hollywood treadmill. In all likelihood, they thought, this show would disappear without a trace, just like so many of their past pilot scripts. Fox surprised them by expressing interest in green-lighting a script, but Warner Bros. was still interested in cutting a deal elsewhere (at the time, Fox was still an upstart with little of the cachet of the other three networks) and scheduled Kauffman and Crane for a meeting with NBC in December 1993.

Warren Littlefield always judged writers by their ability to hold a room. Could they seize control of the dead Burbank air and commandeer it with the power and vigor of their stories? Could they make script characters come to life? To do so was, of course, little guarantee of future success, but Littlefield intuitively felt that being able to convince jaded network executives was a promising down payment toward winning over a skeptical national audience.

Kauffman and Crane had worked with NBC once before, on the short-lived 1992 political farce *The Powers That Be*. The network had been won over by their witty scripts, but Kauffman and Crane had not been the showrunners (Norman Lear of *All in the Family* fame was also involved in the show, as an executive producer), and Littlefield had felt that the show had never lived up to its potential.

As Littlefield and his colleagues sipped water, Kauffman and Crane brought the room to life with their amusing, heartfelt pitch about six Manhattan twentysomethings in search of themselves. They acted out the characters and the scenarios for a show they were calling *Insomnia Café,* allowing the room of network executives to momentarily imagine a crew of friends, swigging coffee and bantering, that felt more like a substitute family.

It was a simple pitch—*Cheers* in a coffee shop—but it was more than that. It felt deeply personal, a transmutation of lived experience into a story that would register with the widest possible swath of viewers. A bell was going off in Littlefield's head, confirming that the nebulous thing he had been in search of since becoming president of NBC had been located. This, finally, was what he wanted.

Kauffman and Crane's series was being produced by Warner Bros., and WB Television's president, Les Moonves, was representing the show's interests in negotiations. Moonves neglected to tell NBC that Fox had already expressed interest in the show, or even that it had been pitched to other networks at all. Moonves, soon to become the president of CBS's entertainment division, told Littlefield that picking up the show would come with certain conditions. Acquiring Kauffman and Crane's series would require a pilot commitment. NBC would have to bypass the script stage, where the network could acquire a single script from the writers and decide whether to proceed to filming a pilot. Filming a poor pilot that did not make it to air would be the equivalent of a $250,000 penalty. NBC would hardly sink under the weight of such a cost, but too many failed pilots could blow a substantial hole in the network's development budget.

For Littlefield, it felt like a reasonable request coming from Moonves and the Warner Bros. team, and there wouldn't be any penalty unless the series wound up a disappointment. Littlefield was confident that the new show would fill one of the slots on their new, youth-oriented Thursday-night lineup, and so the up-front costs of developing the show were simply the price of doing business. Moonves was being aggressive, but NBC wanted to be in business with Warner Bros. on this show and did not want it to end up elsewhere.

NBC made the pilot commitment for *Insomnia Café* and took the show off the market. But Kauffman and Crane remained unsatisfied with the show's title. Their outline for the show was renamed *Bleecker Street*, after the Manhattan street Kauffman had lived on, and the first draft of the pilot script was labeled *NBC Pilot Which Still Needs a Title*.

Littlefield only had one notable tweak he wanted to suggest. He was concerned, he noted to Kauffman and Crane, about how much time their characters were spending in their neighborhood coffee shop. How much action could reasonably take place in a café? Littlefield wanted the characters' apartments to take on more prominence. And if the characters were meant to live in the same apartment building, as the pilot script indicated, Littlefield suggested that the apartment of roommates Joey and Chandler be placed directly across the hall from Rachel and Monica's apartment, allowing some of the action to take place in the hallway between their doors.

Crane thought the note was a solid one. "You could call it *Across the Hall*," Littlefield helpfully suggested. "Or just have it be across the hall," Crane responded, nonplussed by the mediocre title. They still couldn't settle on a decent title for the show. After a temporary interlude where they adopted Littlefield's suggestion, Warner Bros. sponsored an internal name-that-show contest. The big winner was Crane's partner Jeffrey Klarik, who suggested *Friends Like Us*.

———

NBC was mostly hands-off after ordering Kauffman and Crane's pilot, with their notes running to such minor matters as the beige-toned color of the couch in the coffeehouse. (They preferred a less repellent shade.) The one major suggestion the network had for Crane and Kauffman was the addition of an older secondary character. NBC was concerned that if all the main characters were in their twenties, it would distinctly limit the series' breakout appeal. An older character—even one that made only occasional appearances—could convince hesitant older viewers to check in with *Friends Like Us*. Perhaps, the network thought, there might be an older acquaintance they ran into at the coffeehouse who could give them advice about their lives?

It was a poor idea, and while it would not sink the show, it would undoubtedly weaken its spell. Kauffman and Crane reluctantly agreed, and began trying to wedge the character, whom they referred to as "Pat the Cop," after an older police officer who used to hang out in the movie theater where *Dream On* writers Jeff Greenstein and Jeff Strauss used to work in Somerville, Massachusetts, during college, into their next script. The writers made a good-faith attempt, even casting the role, but hated the resulting script so much that they pleaded with NBC to drop the idea. If only NBC would kill Pat the Cop, they promised, they would give their six protagonists parents in notable supporting roles, and find older guest stars to attract a more mature audience. NBC gave its permission, and Pat the Cop was no longer.

The show would live or die on the strength of its six main characters. But who would play the roles?

CHAPTER 2

SIX OF ONE

Casting the Show

Barbara Miller, the head of casting for Warner Bros. Television, handed over a script. "Read this," she told Ellie Kanner, "work on some lists, and you'll meet with David Crane, Marta Kauffman, and Kevin Bright. Be ready!" Kanner, then only twenty-nine, had recently been promoted to casting director, having cast shows like *Step by Step* and *Lois & Clark: The New Adventures of Superman,* and this script would be one of the first she would help to cast at Warner Bros. After reading the script, Kanner was puzzled. Why wasn't everyone else at Warner Bros. as excited about this pilot as she was?

It was a casting director's job to be familiar with most of the young performers in the industry and able to mentally pore over the possibilities and identify strong candidates. Kanner took out her notepad and began making lists of all the funny young performers she knew, breaking them into subcategories for each of the roles in the script: sad-sack divorcé Ross; his luckless-in-love sister, Monica; quirky Phoebe; neurotic Chandler; Chandler's actor roommate, Joey; and Monica's high school friend Rachel. Kanner's assistant Lorna Johnson began calling agencies and checking actors' availabilities. And as Kanner and Johnson were winnowing their list, they were also being sent further candidates by the agencies. Kanner wound up receiving upward of one thousand headshots for each role.

It was February 1994, and Kanner knew she only had about eight weeks to scrutinize her lists, audition the performers she'd selected, narrow it down to about one hundred actors that the producers would see, and help them make their final selections. Actors would be called in for a first audition, where they would read briefly from the script. Kanner would sort through the performances and select a smaller swath of actors who would audition for the showrunners as well. The next step would be to pick a handful of finalists for each role—professionally successful but personally devastated Ross, guitar-playing New Age princess Phoebe, tough-talking "downtown woman" Monica, self-impressed heartthrob Joey, runaway bride Rachel, and sarcastic, witty, perpetually single Chandler—who would be given the opportunity to audition for not only Kanner and the showrunners but Warner Bros. executives as well.

The early casting would be overseen by Kauffman and Bright. Crane had a self-diagnosed tendency to love every actor he saw and had voluntarily removed himself from the first part of the process. He wanted to hire every actor who came in and felt guilty when they couldn't. Crane would be invaluable in the later stages of casting, but it was primarily Kauffman and Bright's task to cull the initial list.

The producers expressed a desire to be open about race and ethnicity as well. They knew that the Ross and Monica characters were to be siblings, and had decided that they would be played by white performers, but were open to anyone for the other four roles. Kanner's initial lists included numerous African-American and Asian-American performers. The flexibility was a step forward, to be sure, but some of *Friends'* later struggles regarding diversity were etched in stone here. Without an explicit desire to cast actors who looked more like New York, the producers were likely going to end up, as if by default, with an all-white cast. As later critics would note, comedy was a less integrated genre than drama. Dramatic series had room for a greater variety of characters, and their settings—hospitals, precinct houses, courtrooms—allowed for characters from different walks of life to interact. Comedy expected its audiences to embrace its characters and was far more tentative about asking them to identify with characters who were not white and middle-class. Television executives were more fearful of asking audiences to laugh along with characters of color, concerned that such shows would be ignored by the majority-white audience.

Kauffman and Crane had their own casting ideas, as well. They had auditioned David Schwimmer on a previous pilot of theirs, called *Couples,* and had loved his work. They had pushed strongly to cast him, but the network had insisted on selecting the other finalist, Jonathan Silverman, instead. Kevin Bright had watched the process, noting the careful language that the network had used, and believed it was a matter of finding Schwimmer too Jewish for network television. The situation was ludicrous, of course; here they were, three Jewish showrunners being forced to select one Jewish actor instead of another one. But Bright suspected that Silverman was seen as a handsome Jew, one who could pass as a leading man, and Schwimmer was not.

Schwimmer had recently attracted glowing reviews for his turn on *NYPD Blue* as creepy neighbor "4B." Schwimmer was a theater kid like Kauffman and Crane, a trained actor with an impressively wide range and a seriousness about the craft that they admired. While they were working on the pilot script for *Friends Like Us,* Kauffman and Crane conferred about the Ross character, remembered the actor they loved but hadn't been able to cast, and said, "David Schwimmer for this."

They envisioned Ross as a highly educated scientist in a crew consisting mostly of working-class strivers. "So his career is pretty together," Kauffman and Crane wrote in their pitch document. "However, when we meet him, he's just signed his divorce papers. . . . His wife left him for his best friend . . . Debbie. He had no idea." Ross would be the "loyal husband" who suddenly found himself excited by the world of available women around him: "It's kind of like he's back in junior high. Only there are no books." Kauffman and Crane pictured an episode where Ross would take a date to the planetarium and woo her under the stars—a plotline that would notably be reused, with a different woman. The pilot would eventually drop the wife-runs-off-with-female-best-friend angle but still retain Ross's wife coming out as a lesbian.

They were ready to offer him the role without his even having to audition—a rare privilege for a young, untested actor. There was only one problem: Schwimmer did not want to do the show. More than that, he did not want to do any more television at all.

Schwimmer had just been on the short-lived Fox comedy series *Monty* (1994), in which he had played the left-wing son of a Rush Limbaugh–esque conservative firebrand, played by *Happy Days'* Henry Winkler, and had found it to be a miserable experience. As he saw it, television was a place where nobody listened to your ideas, where you reported for duty every day to do mediocre, unsatisfying work. When *Monty* was canceled, Schwimmer felt immense relief and immediately returned to Chicago, where he was working on a new theatrical production of *The Master and Margarita*. His theater company, the Lookingglass, had just moved into a new space, and Schwimmer felt like he was in the exact place he wanted to be. He had gotten a buzz cut for the role of Pontius Pilate for the show and was prepared to thrust himself into Mikhail Bulgakov's fantastical world of Soviet totalitarianism tempered with magical realism.

Schwimmer had appeared in a number of pilots that had never gone anywhere, and he found the whole process mystifying and frustrating. What was the point of acting if no one could see your work? He would not, his agent Leslie Siebert told Kanner, be reading any more television scripts. Kauffman and Crane were chagrined but not quite ready to give up on their dream casting.

In the meantime, though, the producers began looking at other actors. The casting process for *Friends Like Us* was moving slowly, and other, faster series began to snatch away talented performers. Kanner brought Noah Wyle in for the role of Ross. The producers liked his audition and wanted him to test for the network, but the pilot was not going to shoot until May. In the meantime, Wyle auditioned for *ER,* also being produced by Warner Bros. that same pilot season, and *Friends Like Us* moved into second position, meaning that they were second in line for the actor's services. If the first show fell through, they would be able to cast him on their series. Wyle, of course, wound up being cast on *ER* instead. Among the other actors who auditioned for Ross was future *Will & Grace* star Eric McCormack, who came in two or three times.

They also considered Mitchell Whitfield, who would eventually be cast as Rachel's ex Barry. Whitfield advanced so far in the process that after one meeting, he received a surreptitious phone call from someone involved with the show who brought good, if inaccurate, news: "Hey, congratulations, they love you for Ross. Looks like you're going to be Ross."

Meanwhile, Siebert had begged Schwimmer to look at the script, telling him that Kauffman and Crane were admirers of his craft. Schwimmer remembered how much he had enjoyed the *Couples* script and was pleased to learn that their new show was to be an ensemble series, with no designated star. This could be a television series that worked a bit more like a theatrical troupe.

Schwimmer had also gotten unexpected phone calls from Robby Benson, the former child star who had become a well-regarded television director, and from James Burrows, the legendary director behind *Taxi* and *Cheers.* Both of them were also telling him that Kauffman and Crane had specifically written the role with him in mind, which Schwimmer had not fully understood beforehand. If these titans of television were suggesting he reconsider, Schwimmer later told Littlefield, he would be an idiot not to go. Schwimmer read the script and agreed to fly out to Los Angeles to meet with them.

Executives from Warner Bros. and NBC filled the edges of the room as Schwimmer picked up the pages of the pilot script. Kanner, who was reading with him, was immediately overcome with the quiet joy of knowing that an actor was perfect for a role. The role of Ross was like an off-the-rack suit that did not require any tailoring for Schwimmer to wear. He could simply put it on. It already fit perfectly. "OK," she told herself, "this was meant to be." Fortunately, Schwimmer agreed and accepted the part.

After Schwimmer was cast, Bright and Kauffman spent weeks fruitlessly looking at actors for the other roles. They would listen to the script, day after day, being mauled by performers who could not locate the comedy trapped inside of it. They began to doubt the value of the script itself. Perhaps they had mistakenly believed it was funnier than it actually was?

One early session was held in Barbara Miller's office. The actors auditioning for *Friends Like Us* were surrounded by photographs of Greta Garbo and Bette Davis, as if to remind them of the legendary work that had been done on this very lot. Actors came fully dressed for the job they wanted, with a passel of Phoebes in nose rings and bell-bottoms, and an array of Joeys displaying ample chest hair. Auditions were a frustrating process, with actors displaying distinct limits to their range or unable to replicate what they had done in an earlier audition. Miller exchanged notes with Kanner, Kauffman, Crane, and the Warner Bros. executives after the session, and everyone agreed that there were only a few performers good enough for the next audition—which would be held at NBC. Some of the performers were too sitcom-y, while others were too theatrical. They would have to keep searching.

Television acting was about graciously accepting the near-inevitability of failure. You would audition for a role, but you would never get it. You would get a role, but the show would never make it to air. The show would make it to air, but it would never find an audience. And even when big breaks arrived, they could vanish without warning.

At Vassar, everyone had thought Lisa Kudrow was a dumb Southern California blonde because she was always smiling, but she had ambitious career plans for herself. She was a biology major, and after graduation, she would work for her father, a migraine specialist, before proceeding to a graduate program in neuroscience. In her spare time, she would turn on the television and catch an episode of a sitcom and be turned off by the ways their performers emoted. "I'd hear the delivery of a line or a joke and I'd think, '[They're] pushing it too hard,'" she would later tell an interviewer. "It just kept happening and so I finally just surrendered and said, 'All right, I'm going to give it a try.'" Kudrow worried about what it might mean to become an actor. They were, in her mind, doing things like appearing on late-night television to ask audiences to save the planet on their behalf and other acts of self-regarding hubris. What would happen to her were she to become a performer as well?

Once Kudrow set out to act, she realized she could use what others mistakenly perceived to be her ditziness to her advantage. Kudrow joined the Groundlings improv troupe, briefly dated future late-night host Conan O'Brien, and took acting lessons. She soon came to understand that feeling the need to apologize for being an actor was an impediment to success. It would be far better to acknowledge that there were countless other actors competing for the same jobs, and that solid work and dedication would eventually carry the day. Being funny was a serious business. It would be enough to maintain your dignity and do your work. Eventually, people would begin to notice.

Kudrow appeared in small roles on *Cheers* and *Mad About You*, and was going out regularly on auditions. *Cheers* had just ended, and Kelsey Grammer was to continue playing Dr. Frasier Crane in a new show called *Frasier*. After wowing the producers during auditions, Kudrow received the opportunity of a lifetime: She was cast as Frasier's radio producer Roz.

Once the show was in rehearsals, cocreator Peter Casey was taken aback by what he was seeing. Kudrow was excellent, but Roz was intended to be a forceful foil to Frasier, able to give as good as she got.

Instead, following each day's run-through, Casey and the writers were modifying the script because Kudrow was not able to be as steely as they had intended Roz to be. And Grammer was playing down his lines because he was concerned that he might overwhelm Kudrow if he performed them as intended.

Casey consulted with James Burrows, the director supervising the series, and they were in agreement: Lisa Kudrow had to be fired. *Frasier* retooled, casting Peri Gilpin, another finalist for the role, as Roz, and Kudrow was convinced that the best opportunity she would ever get as an actor had slipped through her fingers.

A few months later, running perilously low on money, Kudrow got a call from her agent, who was delivering an unusual message. There was an offer of a role that she should turn down. *Mad About You* had called about Kudrow's coming back to play a new part. She would be needed on set in one hour and would not be able to see the script until she arrived. It was, her agent argued, insulting and demeaning.

Kudrow took the job anyway, and did so well that series creator Danny Jacobson immediately offered her a recurring role, with at least five more appearances over the course of the season. One of the people she impressed on *Mad About You* was staff writer Jeffrey Klarik, who proceeded to tell his partner, David Crane, all about the gifted performer playing hapless waitress Ursula. One day, she got a call from Crane, who told her he was casting for his new show and would love to have her come in and read. Would she be interested?

Phoebe was, according to the pitch, "sweet, flaky, a waif, a hippie." Crane and Kauffman pictured her as a free spirit who played bad folk songs on her guitar and dated a lot: "She sees the good in everyone, which is a nice way of saying she's indiscriminate. One week she can be in love with a Japanese businessman, the next week a street mime, the next a fifty-three-year-old butcher." Phoebe would not have her own apartment: "She owns what she can fit in her backpack." The pilot would eventually tone down Phoebe's serial dating while retaining her musical stylings and her flakiness.

When Kudrow arrived, both Kanner and Crane felt an instant buzz telling them she was just right for the part. But they knew that the networks would not be satisfied with only one choice, and so dozens of other actresses tried out for Phoebe as well, including future stars Jane Lynch and Kathy Griffin.

Kudrow went back to work at *Mad About You*, where she was helping many of her friends and fellow guest performers run lines for their auditions. She was struck by the enthusiasm other actors seemed to have for this new show in particular. It seemed like every dramatic actor in Los Angeles was out for a role on *ER*, and every comedic actor was hoping to be cast in Kauffman and Crane's show.

It wound up being another month until Kudrow was called back to test for the role. While she waited, Kudrow had had ample time to think over the part of Phoebe. The day before the test, Kudrow's agent called Kanner, frantic. "Look. Lisa is thinking about a different way to do the audition with you tomorrow at the network," she told Kanner. "And she just wants to run it by you."

Kanner knew from experience that time was often not the actor's friend. Actors granted too much time to ponder their performance might tweak it excessively, coming in with a take on a role so radically changed from their first attempt that the producers could no longer see what had appealed to them at first.

Kudrow was wise enough to know that she might be about to stumble and asked if she could first appear in front of just Kanner and Kauffman. They agreed, and she came in to offer her new version of Phoebe. It was fine, but it lacked the brilliant flakiness they had loved about her first attempt. Kauffman and Kanner looked at each other, and Kanner said, "No no no no no, go back to the original way. That was what we want. That will get you this job." "OK, great," Kudrow responded, unruffled. "I just wanted to double-check." She went back to her original take and got offered the role.

Kudrow was excited about playing Phoebe but concerned that a failed series might do damage to her recurring role on *Mad About You*.

She was relieved that *Friends Like Us* was going to be on NBC, meaning that her two series shared a network. "Pilots work and don't work," she told the NBC executives, "but we have to protect *Mad About You,* please." Kudrow did not want a failed pilot to mean the end of her role on *Mad About You.*

The biggest star the producers were considering for the show was *Family Ties* veteran Courteney Cox. Kanner originally had Cox on her list for Rachel, which she believed would be the best fit for an essentially sweet performer like Cox. Monica, who was not yet cast, they envisioned as an edgier role. The producers were looking for someone slightly less glamorous who could potentially play a harried, occasionally bitter everywoman.

Monica was to be "tough, defended, cynical, sarcastic." In an ultra-nineties reference, they described her as having "the attitude of Sandra Bernhard or Rosie O'Donnell and the looks of Duff," referring to the MTV VJ and model Karen Duffy. Monica, in this original conception, was to be a blue-collar New Yorker with aspirations of starting her own restaurant. She would work at a Le Cirque–like establishment: "We just think it would be fun to see this tough, downtown woman in this uptown, French bullshit arena." Monica would also have a "real maternal side," looking after Rachel and adopting a pregnant woman who would end up giving birth in her apartment. Monica dreamed of becoming a mother but first found herself in search of a man to have children with.

When Kauffman and Crane had written the role, they had pictured the dialogue emerging from the mouth of Janeane Garofalo, who had the snarky attitude and comic bite that they envisioned for Monica. They offered her the role, but Garofalo turned them down, preferring to join the cast of *Saturday Night Live* instead. Kauffman and Crane were unsure where to turn next.

Cox came in and read for Rachel, and was excellent. Afterward, Cox requested to come back and read for Monica as well, and Kanner acquiesced. Cox was good as Monica—a definite maybe—but the producers knew they wanted her as Rachel.

They had already brought in hundreds of performers for Monica, including future stars like Leah Remini (*The King of Queens*). The producers were now strongly considering Nancy McKeon, another 1980s sitcom star, familiar to audiences as Jo from *The Facts of Life*.

Kauffman and Crane were confident enough that Cox was right for Rachel that they were willing to offer her a test option deal, which gave her a guarantee of the role without another audition. Courteney Cox would be Rachel, and casting for Monica would carry on. Cox told them she was glad for the offer but really preferred the role of Monica.

Kanner and the producers agreed to let her read again for Monica, figuring all along that they would offer her the part of Rachel immediately after the audition and that the excitement of being cast would win out over any lingering preference for the role of Monica. Instead, Cox came in and absolutely nailed it as Monica. "Holy crap!" Kanner thought to herself. "She's great as Monica! Why didn't we see that before?"

Where Kudrow had gone off and returned with a performance less charming than her original version of Phoebe, Cox had clearly returned with a vastly improved Monica. She had committed to her vision of the role and had won over Kanner and the skeptical producers, who had initially been unable to see her in any role but Rachel's. Cox's casting turned the show away from its initial concept of Monica as a working-class interloper in an upper-crust sphere, and she was retooled as more middle-class and suburban. Now Monica was set—but casting Rachel was the new puzzle.

Meanwhile, the role of Joey had been described, in the casting call for actors, as a "handsome, smug macho guy in his 20s" with a passion for "women, sports, women, New York, women." The pitch referred to Joey as having moved to New York from Chicago to "become an actor. Well, to become Al Pacino." Joey "really thinks he's god's gift to women," but Monica in particular resolutely refuses to be charmed by his charms. Kauffman and Crane pictured Monica and Joey as foils for each other, squabbling about whether men are intimidated by Monica because she is a strong woman or because she is a "bitch." (Kauffman would later make reference to never using the word *bitch* on the show, but it does appear in the pitch document itself.) Joey acts in children's theater, which he finds unfulfilling, and works a variety of gigs to make the rent, including bouncer, bike messenger, and "the guy in the department store saying 'Aramis? Aramis? Aramis?'"

Kauffman and Crane sat through more than fifty prospective Joeys, including future guest star Hank Azaria, making their way through the lines they were handed—a monologue debunking the idea that there is only one woman for any given man. Women, Joey would observe, were like flavors of ice cream—each delicious in her own way. Writing those lines had brought up a certain sound. There was a pacing and delivery that Kauffman and Crane imagined for Joey, and no one yet had captured it.

Crane and Kauffman initially pictured Joey and Monica as the central romantic couple for the show. Joey, the perpetual horndog, would be lured, and possibly tamed, by the warm, affectionate Monica. In this initial version, Joey was less dim-witted than he would eventually become, with an emphasis on his ladies'-man style and his city-boy attitude. Initially, the casting search was for more of a leading-man type. Crane was taken aback to find that this approach led Joey to feel more boring than they had expected him to be. None of the actors they brought in to audition conveyed the charm they had in mind. As it stood, Joey felt as if he did not belong in this particular circle of friends.

Casting assistant Stacy Alexander had brought Kanner a tape of an actor who had begun to make a name for himself on low-rent Fox comedy series like *Married . . . with Children*, *Top of the Heap*, and *Vinnie & Bobby*. The material was notably different, but there was something about Matt LeBlanc that could possibly work for the role of Joey. "He could be perfect," thought Kanner.

Matt LeBlanc had been born to a working-class family in the ritzy Boston suburb of Newton. LeBlanc grew up in a household run by his mother and did not meet his father, a Vietnam veteran, until he was eight years old.

He was in love with the roar and flash of motorcycles and sports cars, something he shared with his mechanic father. LeBlanc dreamed of success as a motorcycle racer and spent his leisure hours participating in youth racing events. He studied to be a carpenter but found the profession too staid for his more adventurous tastes. At eighteen, LeBlanc left Newton for New York, intent on pursuing a career as a model but was repeatedly told he was too short.

One day, LeBlanc was walking down the street when he paused to check out a beautiful woman's butt. As it happened, she had paused to check out *his* butt, and the two laughed about their undisguised attraction. She told him she was an actress and was on the way to an audition. Why didn't he come and meet her manager? LeBlanc agreed, and an impromptu career in acting was launched. He soon won roles in television commercials. LeBlanc was the intrepid young man in the Heinz commercial who placed a ketchup bottle at the edge of a building so he could drizzle it onto his hot dog on the street below.

LeBlanc came in for an audition for the role of Joey, and the producers were charmed. He had been running lines the previous day with a fellow actor, and, inspired by the script's celebration of friendship, they had gone out for a drink together. LeBlanc, having perhaps gotten a bit too friendly, fell down and scraped his nose. When he came in to read, Kauffman asked what had happened to his face, and LeBlanc, replying, "Aw, it's a long story," launched into a description of his night on the town. Kauffman laughed at the story, and LeBlanc felt that the audition had suddenly tilted in his favor.

LeBlanc was not nearly as experienced as some of the other actors they were considering, but he had the remarkable capacity to continue improving each time they came back to him. He could naturally pull off the machismo and arrogance of Joey, but he also had an appealing sweetness to him. LeBlanc had the rare gift of likability. Even when Joey was saying something that might come off as hateful emerging from another character's mouth, LeBlanc was able to make it seem charming.

They decided to bring him back for a test and ultimately offered him the role of Joey.

After LeBlanc's audition, Crane and Kauffman began to rethink the role. Joey was still an actor, but he would now come with an outer-borough, working-class demeanor. The changes meant that it no longer made quite so much sense to have Joey and Monica as the central couple. That role was now open to be filled by other characters. LeBlanc himself had pushed for Joey to be more like a big brother to his female friends, never attempting to woo any of them. Kauffman thought the idea of Joey and Monica had made sense on the page, but once Cox and LeBlanc were cast, it no longer did.

Meanwhile, other roles were trickier to fill. The surprise switch to Monica for Cox had left the character of Rachel open once more. Crane thought the role of Rachel was an exceedingly tough one. He and Kauffman intended Rachel to be charming and warm and modestly clueless, but he worried that, in the wrong hands, she might become incredibly unlikable. Crane did not want Rachel to be perceived as a spoiled, petulant, husband-abandoning mess and needed the right actress who would telegraph Rachel's more attractive personality traits.

Rachel was described as someone who had belatedly come to a realization about her own life: "What happened was, she was in the room with all the presents, looking at the gravy boat, this gorgeous china gravy boat, and she realized she was more turned on by the gravy boat than by Barry, the man she's about to marry. So she got really freaked out and got high with Mindy, her maid of honor, and while she was getting high she realized that Barry looks an awful lot like Mr. Potato Head. She always knew he looked familiar. So she had to get out of there." Rachel was a young woman who unexpectedly had to start over again: "She decides to move to the city because she knows if she stays in Teaneck and she doesn't marry Barry, she'll marry Gary or Larry."

Numerous actors, including *Saved by the Bell*'s Elizabeth Berkley, had come in to read for the part. Kanner liked an experienced young actress named Jennifer Aniston, who had starred in an ill-fated television adaptation of *Ferris Bueller's Day Off* on NBC in 1990–91. Kanner was charmed by Aniston, but she was already committed to another series. Aniston's series *Muddling Through*, picked up by CBS, had already shot eight episodes, and while they had yet to air it—generally the kiss of death for a new series—they still retained the right to do so. And if they did, Aniston would remain contractually obligated to the series.

Kanner decided to take the risk and have Aniston come in to read in second position. This meant that NBC did not have first dibs on Aniston, whose availability would be dependent on *Muddling Through's* getting canceled. When Crane and Kauffman first saw Aniston, they fell in love with her, rooting for Rachel to find her footing in spite of herself. Jennifer Aniston could be the heart of their series.

She had to lose thirty pounds if she wanted to stay in Hollywood. Los Angeles was a tough place to be an actress—it was a tough place to be a woman—and Jennifer Aniston's agent was reluctantly leveling with her. She had been called back for an audition, and this time, she was requested to arrive in a leotard and tights. "This'll blow it for me," she joked with her agent, and was surprised when he responded seriously. Aniston was hardly fat—everyone could see she was beautiful—but as the show she would one day become indelibly associated with later made a point of noting, the camera added ten pounds, and if Aniston wanted to be competitive for television roles, she would have to slim down.

Hollywood was a tough business, but Jennifer Aniston had known this her entire life. Her father, John Aniston, was an actor who had spent years as a featured performer on the soap opera *Search for Tomorrow*. Her godfather was none other than Kojak himself, Telly Savalas. Acting was a struggle. It took years for John Aniston to make a steady living from it. He had been selling vacuum cleaners door-to-door, subsisting on the occasional acting job Savalas could toss his way.

Her parents divorced when Aniston was nine years old, and her father was suddenly a ghost in their own home, an absence. She would sneak peeks of *Search for Tomorrow* to catch a glimpse of him. Aniston would record the dialogue of shows like *Joanie Loves Chachi* on cassettes and then play them in her room, seeing what it felt like to pretend to be Joanie.

When she was twenty, Aniston moved to Los Angeles. Aniston was pretty and sweet and unthreatening, and Hollywood liked her for roles as younger sisters and bratty upstarts on shows like *Ferris Bueller* and *Molloy,* which lasted for all of seven episodes. *Friends Like Us* was an opportunity to play a more significant leading-woman role, and she wanted it badly.

Crane knew that Aniston was committed to *Muddling Through* and decided to approach its showrunner to see if he would release her so she could join the *Friends Like Us* cast. In retrospect, Crane could not believe his own audacity. How would he have responded if the showrunner from some other show asked him to release one of the actors they had worked so hard to find so they could star in some entirely different show? Crane was politely but firmly turned down. Aniston made her own efforts to escape, approaching Leslie Moonves and crying to him about the situation in the hopes that he would help her escape her CBS straitjacket. This, too, did not work.

Ellie Kanner was about to leave for a much-needed vacation when she received a telephone call telling her that *Muddling Through* had been picked up by CBS. The Tiffany Network was getting to not only express its optimism in one of its own series but also potentially blow a giant hole in its rival's schedule.

Kanner was told it was time to recast the role of Rachel. She proceeded to spend the next month looking at head shots and overseeing auditions, but no one captivated her the way Aniston had. The role was offered to Téa Leoni, who was a superlative actor and comedian but might have come off as too sophisticated to play a role like Rachel.

Leoni turned the role down, and the network soon called Crane, summarily informing him that Rachel had been offered to Jami Gertz, a sitcom veteran from *Square Pegs* and *The Facts of Life* who had also appeared on *Dream On*. Crane had always liked Gertz but believed she was wrong for Rachel. Moreover, Gertz was a Sabbath-observant Jew, and she asked the showrunners to commit to a Wednesday-to-Tuesday schedule, where shoots would take place on Tuesday nights, and not Friday nights, as with many other shows. The showrunners respected Gertz's commitment (Bright would later call her "the Sandy Koufax of show business") but could not lock themselves into such an arrangement.

They also shared with Gertz their conception of the show as an ensemble, lacking a single star, and were under the impression that she was looking for a series that could serve as more of a vehicle. Crane and Kauffman sweated out the lengthy wait until the next day, when Gertz passed on the show. They were relieved that they had not yet lost control of casting their series.

Eventually, CBS and NBC negotiated a temporary détente. CBS would allow Aniston to be cast in both series but would unambiguously retain first position for their show. Aniston would be able to shoot the first six episodes of *Friends Like Us*. But if the CBS series was picked up, *Friends Like Us* would lose Aniston midway through the season. It was an enormous risk.

———

Kauffman and Crane knew what they were in search of for the role of Chandler. The character had a certain timbre to the way his lines should be delivered, and they were hoping to find a performer who could capture the music in their heads. Crane thought it would be the easiest role to cast, consisting almost exclusively of a string of jokes to be rattled off. And yet no one could quite capture the sound they were looking for.

Chandler was to be "the droll observer of everybody else's life. And his own." He was an office drone who knows his job is "killing his brain cells and his sperm. But it's a place to make long distance calls from." Chandler was a romantic sad sack with "a knack for finding women who turn out wierd [*sic*]." They would be the type who "wants to play the girl scout and the man who won't buy the cookies. Or another wants him to accept her Lord. A Lord that none of us is familiar with."

Chandler was a self-consciously comic role—a character who believed himself to be funny and used humor as a protective mechanism—and required an actor who could sell both the humor and the damaged self-confidence. In the first wave of actors coming in to read for Chandler, only one actor seemed to grasp what he should sound like: a twenty-four-year-old Canadian named Matthew Perry. Perry had appeared on *Dream On,* and he had an innate comic flair and a truly remarkable gift for delivering each line in an unexpected fashion.

Perry, though, was also already committed to another series: the futuristic ABC sitcom *LAX 2194.* Perry was to star alongside Ryan Stiles and Kelly Hu in a show about futuristic airport employees. Stiles was a robot customs agent and Hu his exasperated human partner, with Perry in a supporting role as a baggage handler tasked with sorting aliens' luggage. It simply could not be possible to come up with a more ludicrous sitcom premise, nor to find one less likely to ever make it to air, but Perry, whose business manager had just informed him that he was flat broke, had begged his agents to find him any work, and *LAX 2194* it was.

Kauffman, Crane, and Bright were at a loss as to how to proceed. Perry was clearly the best performer they had seen, but they could not have him. And Warner Bros. refused to allow them to place any more actors in second position at this point, meaning that Perry was entirely off the table.

Kauffman and Crane saw numerous actors, including Jon Favreau, and had also been impressed by a young actor named Craig Bierko. He was not quite Perry's equal, but the casting process was often a matter of compromise, and Bierko's mien reminded the producers of Perry. NBC had signed Bierko to a deal, and they were intent on finding a role for him in an NBC series. The network pressured Kauffman, Crane, and

Bright to cast Bierko as Chandler. They brought Bierko back for another audition and wound up offering him the role.

Bright was despondent at the thought of Bierko's being on their show. He was a terrific performer and a superlative actor, but he was not Chandler. Bright believed he lacked the instinctive comic pop that such a showy role demanded. He could not credibly convey the acerbic, sarcastic, self-deprecating, but surprisingly lovable persona that they were looking for in Chandler. Bierko was, by all accounts, a pleasure to work with. He just was not right for this particular role.

Bierko, too, had his doubts. He was looking for a starring role, not a part in an ensemble. Bierko wound up turning down *Friends Like Us*. Years later, Bright would receive a letter from Bierko, in which he expressed his realization that in turning down the part of Chandler, he had missed out on the role of a lifetime.

Later, the showrunners found out that Bierko had been practicing for the role by running his lines with another actor: Matthew Perry. Bierko was a talented actor and would go on to have an impressive career in series like *UnREAL*, but Kauffman and Crane realized that what they liked about him for the role of Chandler was merely a reflection of Matthew Perry, and that Bierko had been tutored by Perry to play the role as he would have. They learned that Perry liked the role of Chandler so much that he was coaching numerous other actors on how to play the part.

It was mid-April, and they were still looking to cast the role of Chandler. Crane began to wonder if the fault did not lie in their own writing. Was Chandler simply a poorly written role? Then there was some good news from Warner Bros. WB executive David Janollari had seen the pilot of *LAX 2194* and returned with a verdict: There was absolutely no chance of its making it to air on ABC. "Look," Janollari said, "I know he's not available, but I think he's great as Chandler, and he should go as second position." Kanner was not senior enough to make that call, but Janollari could, and so Kanner, with a sense of relief, agreed: "Great, I'll get him in."

Perry could be called back for a second audition. Crane felt the cartoon sweat flying off him, an expression of his overwhelming relief at having an actor he felt was up to the task of playing Chandler. Perry was brought in to read with Aniston, Cox, and LeBlanc, with another actor filling in for David Schwimmer as Ross. Perry impressed the producers once more with his ability to find a fresh method of delivering Chandler's lines, and they knew that no other performer would come as close to what they imagined their character would sound like.

Normally, a casting director was merely supposed to usher the actor out of the room, murmuring sweet nothings like "good job" but not offering any more information about casting. After Perry finished his audition, Kanner asked him to wait for a moment while she conferred with the producers. Everyone compared notes, and there was unanimous agreement that Perry was so superb there was no way anyone else could play the role. Kanner ran out of the room, pointed to Perry, and gave him a thumbs-up. Perry was shocked: "What?! Really? What?" Kanner had the rare pleasure of immediately sharing life-changing news with an actor she had championed: "Yeah, you got the job!"

After Perry joined the cast, the business-affairs department at NBC approached Littlefield and warned him that the role of Rachel needed to be recast. It was simply too great a risk to leave a promising show like *Friends Like Us* open to sabotage or self-destruction when it could so easily be avoided. Warner Bros. asked Littlefield if he was willing to cover the costs for reshoots if Aniston wound up being unavailable, and he said he would. Littlefield was cognizant of how important good casting could be for the future success of a show and was willing to take a major risk in order to keep the most preferred version of the cast together. But Littlefield also had a plan. He was going to call Preston Beckman.

Muddling Through had already shot a half-dozen episodes, none of which had aired, and CBS, after some dithering, ultimately chose to put the show on its summer schedule, in the relative dead zone of Saturday nights. Hearing the news, Littlefield turned to Beckman, NBC's scheduling guru, with a two-word order: "Kill it."

Beckman returned with a crafty suggestion for eliminating *Muddling Through*'s prospects. Beckman was sitting on a trove of unreleased original TV films adapted from Danielle Steel novels. They were practically guaranteed to attract a substantial, and substantially female, audience. If they were to be scheduled opposite *Muddling Through*? Well, no show about an ex-con motel manager and her daffy family was likely to provide stiff competition for Steel's glamorous romances.

Beckman would schedule the Steel movies for the first few Saturday nights *Muddling Through* was on the air, with repeats scheduled for the weeks that followed. It was a necessary sacrifice, giving up some of the ratings the movies might have garnered on another, more attractive night in exchange for eliminating a rival to potential future Thursday-night success.

In private, Littlefield was scared to death. Losing Aniston would mean millions of dollars in reshoots and recasting. But a network president knew what a rare thing it was to feel the chemistry between performers. Something unique was brewing, and Littlefield felt he would have to be a fool to tamper with what was developing. He would just have to wait for CBS to fold.

The mood in the room on the Warner Bros. lot at the end of April was tense, and more than a little awestruck. To be cast on a network show was a thrill, even if the show, like most others, would almost inevitably fail. But to be working with James Burrows, the man who had shepherded the likes of *Taxi* and *Cheers* to unprecedented heights of artistic and ratings triumph, was to know that the possibility of success had drastically increased, and that there was an unquestioned master of the sitcom arts present at the first read-through of the *Friends Like Us* pilot script.

Burrows made a habit of going through the pilot scripts that his agent would send him each spring. Of all the shows he received for the 1994–95 season, the one that jumped out at him was *Friends Like Us*. Its professional polish appealed to him, as did the clever way in which it managed to introduce a passel of new characters with relatively little strain. Burrows agreed to direct the pilot. His presence alone was significant to the future prospects of the show; being able to say, "Jimmy thinks this is great," vastly improved the odds of its making it to the air in the fall.

The six actors selected by Bright, Kauffman, and Crane said their hellos and gathered around the conference-room table. They opened to the first pages of their scripts and began to read the lines, and Bright relaxed almost immediately. Often with a pilot, there was a sense of fumbling confusion on a first pass through a script. Everyone was exceedingly polite and cautious, and whatever comedy lurked in the script was stepped on by a lack of familiarity with the material. But something remarkable was happening as they read the story of the runaway bride and the lovesick divorcé and their crew of pals. People were laughing. More than that: People were cracking up.

Unlike on some of the other shows Burrows had worked on, the actors on *Friends Like Us* had never all read together before, and so there had been no way to confirm that this experiment would work. Two gifted actors might fail to find a way to coexist on camera, and a promising script might fall flat when performed. These actors appeared to have known each other their whole lives. Burrows nodded to himself, his belief that something unusual was taking place confirmed. Chills were running down Kauffman's spine as they read. This was something extraordinary.

Burrows saw his mission, at this early stage, as encouraging the actors to walk the comic plank for him. He would remind them that the creative process included them and ask them to make suggestions of their own. "Don't just say the words," he told them, "act the words." Burrows would not come into rehearsal with set ideas, would not have spent his evenings moving dolls around a proscenium at home to plan the blocking for a scene. He wanted to be inspired by what his actors did, wanted to oversee a fluid creative process in which his actors peppered him with off-the-cuff ideas and he helped them edit those ideas into a coherent whole.

Burrows wanted the actors, above all, to understand they had the right to create. The actors were themselves taken aback by what their new castmates had come up with. Lisa Kudrow had been sure, after reading the script, that Chandler would be gay and was surprised by Matthew Perry's more hetero take on the character.

He also encouraged them to use physical action to shape the scene. If Ross was pleased with himself for speaking up to Rachel about his feelings, Burrows suggested that Schwimmer might pop the cookie he was holding into his mouth as a capper to the moment.

Kudrow was more than a little cowed by the presence of the man who had worked with Ted Danson, Marilu Henner, and Mary Tyler Moore. She wanted to impress Burrows, and so when he asked her to try a line while hiding under the conference-room table, she gamely crawled underneath and began croaking out her lines. Kauffman and Crane ambled by as Kudrow was perched on the floor, and they reluctantly approached the actress. Phoebe, they suggested, might not handle this scene in quite that fashion. Burrows jumped in to say that he was the one who had suggested it, and Kudrow, relieved, felt assured that she would not be fired—at least not yet.

Of all the performers, the only one anyone might have recognized on the street was Cox, who had made a splashy debut a decade prior as the fresh-faced fan Bruce Springsteen pulls onstage to dance with him in his iconic "Dancing in the Dark" music video. Cox had been raised in the tony Birmingham, Alabama, suburb of Mountain Brook and had plans for a career as an architect upon starting at Mount Vernon College. She wound up dropping out of school to become a model, and won campaigns for Noxzema and Tampax. Cox was the first person to ever use the word *period* in the context of women's health on American television. Cox had built a successful career as a model, even though she had been considered too short for the profession, and she dreamed of establishing a beachhead in acting next.

After "Dancing," she spent two years on *Family Ties* as Michael J. Fox's girlfriend. When the show ended, Cox expected to be vaulted into the stratosphere and instead found herself in search of a big break that was tardy in arriving. She guest-starred on *Dream On* and *Seinfeld*, among other shows, but it was the 1994 film *Ace Ventura: Pet Detective* that finally gave her the opportunity to display her comic chops. She was the straight man to unhinged animal lover Jim Carrey, demonstrating she could hold her own in the wildest situations.

There was an unconscious deference around the table to Cox, as the closest thing the show had to a star. But Cox immediately set the tone for what was to come when she told her fellow cast members that if they had any notes for her, any suggestions about how she might improve her performance, she would be thrilled to hear them. This would be a show about six performers, not one star, and anything that might benefit the quality of the show would be welcomed.

Over the week of working through the script before filming the pilot, Bright watched as the cast grew more comfortable with the material and with each other and began to settle into the roles they had been selected for. Bright believed that they could have simply turned the cameras on for the first run-through and come away with an impressive show.

Nonetheless, the network was unsure about what it had. After a later, less impressive run-through, NBC West Coast president Don Ohlmeyer said he found the show confusing. There were too many characters to follow and too many story lines. This should be a show about Monica, since Courteney Cox was the only star they had. All the other characters should be relegated to secondary status. When Ohlmeyer finished speaking, James Burrows spoke up: "Well, that's not the show I signed on to do." The network's note was dropped. Burrows's word remained gospel.

Burrows was also studying the actors as they worked together, waiting to see what might unfold between them. He was looking for what he thought of as "the unspoken word"—a kind of extrasensory perception that sometimes developed between two gifted performers, in which they could convey an entire array of emotions through the tilt of their shoulders, the angle of their eyebrows, the way their eyes would meet or shy away. It was not necessarily that David Schwimmer and Jennifer Aniston were the most gifted members of the cast—it was increasingly clear that *Friends Like Us* had not made a single misstep in the casting process—but that something profound and unexpected happened when the two actors occupied the screen together.

Traditionally, Burrows would bring in a studio audience about four days into the preparations for the pilot. They would watch what he and the actors had worked out, like a dress rehearsal for a Broadway show, and Burrows would be able to assess how much progress they had made. The audience response was through the roof, instantly reminding Burrows of *Cheers* and *Frasier*. This could be the start of something special.

CHAPTER 3

GRAB A SPOON

Making the Pilot

Having knocked out a first draft of the pilot, Kauffman and Crane called on some of their friends to assist in punching up their script. It was a standard practice in Hollywood for writers to offer a few days' unpaid labor on tightening and improving a pilot. Sometimes, there might be work to be had if the show made it to air; sometimes, those same friends could be asked for help when the time came to write your own show. Kauffman and Crane turned to a trusted inner circle for assistance: Crane's partner, Jeffrey Klarik; and the team of Jeff Greenstein and Jeff Strauss. Greenstein and Strauss had been neophyte writers, scrabbling a living out of writing freelance episodes of the likes of *Charles in Charge* and *Mr. Belvedere,* when they were hired as staff writers on *Dream On.* They had all been ushered into the inner sanctum of television success together and had simultaneously received their joint educations in the business.

When Kauffman and Crane left *Dream On* after its fourth season to sign a deal with Warner Bros., Strauss and Greenstein graduated from being baby writers to showrunners. They oversaw *Dream On's* fifth season, with guidance from Kauffman and Crane as consultants. Kauffman and Crane had served as their mentors in television writing, so it only made sense that when they were developing new shows, Greenstein and Strauss would gladly offer their time. In the spring of 1994, the pair assisted with punching up both *Reality Check* and *Friends Like Us*.

When the pilot was originally laid out, Kauffman and Crane pictured it as centering around a romantic couple whose ebb and flow would be the source of much of the show's comedy and serve as its emotional core, with Monica finding herself drawn to the slovenly, womanizing actor Joey.

After casting the show, Kauffman and Crane wisely stood back and watched their new troupe of actors interact, and were immediately struck by the intensity of the scenes that put together David Schwimmer and Jennifer Aniston. There was something about them—some fascinating, indescribable admixture of attraction and loathing and tenderness and brutishness—that was unlike anything they had ever seen before. The air was charged with anticipation, an empty space that could be creatively filled by the audience. Monica and Joey were no longer, but what about Ross and Rachel? Kauffman and Crane knew that there had to be a lot more of them together, and reimagined the central romantic plotline of the show as being one serving Ross and Rachel.

The pilot, now called *Six of One*, was filmed on the Warner Bros. lot in early May. It was just four months after the Northridge earthquake, and the ground was still occasionally rattling from unexpected tremors, remnants of the 6.7 quake. The night of the pilot's filming, Kevin Bright was relieved and glad to have someone like James Burrows present to oversee the shoot. Burrows was so professional and efficient that the potentially terrifying aspect of shooting a pilot—that so much was riding on this one twenty-two-minute demonstration—was muted.

Burrows was blazingly fast—something that Bright and his colleagues would eventually take exception to—and he made sure to get a loose, witty, exuberant version of the script on film. The tone was a reminder of an essential tenet of Burrows's: Anger was never funny. Anger was a distraction for a comedy. Frustration had a comedic vigor that anger never did, and the trick was always to stay on the side of frustration and never of anger.

Burrows, the one true sitcom veteran among the creative team, was concerned about wearing out the jokes. The audience would be fired up between scenes by a stand-up comedian, but doing too many takes of the same scene would deliver diminishing returns. Burrows had been trained in the theater. He believed that if you wanted to see a second take, you should buy a second ticket, and he directed accordingly. Even still, the process, with camera and lighting resets, was slow enough that some of the audience trickled out before the shoot was complete.

The pilot crisply and subtly laid out much of what would come. It began in the hub of the show's social life, the Central Perk coffee shop. (Much later, Phoebe would gaze at the sign in the window, smile broadly, and say, "I just got that!") Each of the six protagonists was given a brief opportunity to introduce themselves. Chandler shared an anxiety dream from the previous night. He was back in school, flummoxed to find himself naked. Worse, his penis had been replaced by a telephone: "All of a sudden, the phone starts to ring and it turns out it's my mother, which is very, very weird, because she never calls me!" ("One word for you: therapy," another character had told Chandler in the initial outline of the pilot.)

Ross enters the coffee shop, a rain cloud metaphorically perched over his head. Joey spots him and offers a succinct summary of Ross's current mental health: "This guy says, hello, I want to kill myself." Ross has recently been left by his ex-wife, Carol, who has come out as a lesbian, and his friends are curious as to how he could have missed the warning signs. "She didn't know," he replies, "how should I know?"

Chandler, already marked by his Oedipal fixation and fears of castration, sees the story of Ross and Carol as yet another reminder of his own romantic failings: "Sometimes I wish I was a lesbian . . . did I say that out loud?" Both Ross and Chandler are presented as anxious neurotics, with Ross lamenting the loss of his romantic sureties and

Chandler acknowledging that he has never had anything of the kind. Ross's sister, Monica, anxiously preparing herself for a date, and eccentric Phoebe round out the ensemble. (In the initial outline, Monica had started off the episode by describing how she never wanted to go on another date again, and then caved when Phoebe offered to lend her a black dress.)

Ross completes his barrage of woes, which we suspect his friends have heard more than once before, with a lone wish: "I just want to be married again." And at that very moment, the final member of the sextet makes her entrance, her wedding veil streaming over her bare shoulders. Rachel Green (Jennifer Aniston) is now the wish fulfillment of Ross's nuptial fantasy, a bride summoned out of the depths of his psyche to restore him to marital fullness. (Chandler spots Rachel and, hoping for similar success, says, "And I just want a million dollars!") The original *Bleecker Street* script had included Ross's crush on Rachel but relegated it to a secondary plotline, behind Monica's bad date and Rachel's tempestuous arrival at singlehood. Now, with Aniston and Schwimmer cast, and their chemistry so palpable, it occupied center stage.

The ensuing scene is a master class in smooth and efficient storytelling, a compressed love story hidden in the ruffles of Rachel's wedding gown. The show would be sensational in its use of props as a physical expression of fleeting or emotional frames of mind, and it begins here with a sophisticated dirty joke. As Ross haltingly attempts to say hello to Rachel, his umbrella accidentally flies open. Ross's excitement is uncontrollable, visible for all to see, and a source of mild embarrassment. We grasp an elemental truth about him instantly and wordlessly, communicated solely through physical comedy.

Rachel, as it turns out, is an old high school friend of Monica's from Long Island. (Initially, her last name was to have been Robbins, not Green.) Rachel was set to marry Barry (Mitchell Whitfield), her dentist swain, but the sight of a Limoges gravy boat helped her decide at the last minute that a life of wedded bliss was not for her. She and Monica had drifted apart—Monica notes that she was not invited to Rachel's wedding, which her friend acknowledges with a wince—but when Rachel found herself fleeing her life, she instantly thought of Monica.

Rachel and Ross are nudged forward as twin wounded spirits fleeing, or summarily excluded from, the paradise of marriage. Rachel soon finds herself back at Monica's apartment, calling her father to explain her rash decision: "It's like, all of my life, everyone has always told me, 'You're a shoe, you're a shoe, you're a shoe, you're a shoe.' And then today, I just stopped and I said, 'What if I don't want to be a shoe? What if I want to be a purse, you know? Or a hat?'"

Rachel is pegged as a spoiled Jewish American Princess type, on the cusp of leaping from her father's care to her husband's when she suddenly pauses, hesitating. She goes on to tell her father that she might not need his money anymore, only to step back, shocked, from her own self-created precipice: "Wait, wait! I said maybe!"

Joey, with a mop-top do and a black leather jacket to telegraph alpha-male vigor (he has already hit on Rachel, telling her he lives across the hall and that his roommate, Chandler, is often away), pulls Ross aside and, making use of the lines trotted out during auditions, compares women to flavors of ice cream. You could order rocky road or cookie dough, you could ask for sprinkles or whipped cream. "Welcome back to the world!" he tells Ross. "Grab a spoon!" "I honestly don't know if I'm hungry or horny," Ross responds.

Rachel, left to her own devices, finds herself sobbing over Joanie and Chachi's wedding from *Happy Days* (itself an echo of Aniston's childhood habit of recording *Joanie Loves Chachi*). Rachel will never be one of those radiant sitcom brides, she is realizing, and her rash decision has thrust her into an unfamiliar place whose rules are entirely foreign to her. "I'm gonna go get," she haltingly decides, stumbling over her words, "one of those job things." Rachel is not quite ready to cut the cord, though. In the next scene, she exultantly sways into Central Perk, showing off her latest purchase—a gleaming pair of boots, bought with her father's credit card.

Monica, still not entirely formed at this early stage (her plotline in the pilot revolves around a date with a caddish guy), is primarily present as a foil and mentor for Rachel. Monica hugs Rachel after she cuts up her father's credit cards, telling her, "Welcome to the real world. It sucks. You're gonna love it."

Bright was intent on *Six of One*'s having a more cinematic feel than most television series. In the bittersweet moment when lovelorn Rachel was gazing out the window, Bright wanted a close-up of Aniston from outside the window—generally a sitcom no-no. He had prepared a temporary fourth wall, but Burrows bristled at the thought of such a composition.

Bright wanted to see Rachel's face in the window and was willing to put in the work to ensure that they could do it. "I need it," he told Burrows. "I've got to have that shot." Burrows reluctantly agreed, and set up and executed the shot so quickly that Bright almost missed it entirely. "All right!" bellowed Burrows. "That's it. We're moving on." It was not really the shot Bright had asked for. He would have to blow it up to get the full close-up he was hoping for, but it was at least the right actor from the right angle. It would do.

The pilot establishes another of the show's abiding interests: mining the past for comic and interpersonal insight. For it turns out that Ross—Monica's older brother—has also known Rachel for years. As Rachel pours her heart out at the coffee shop, Ross is silently pouring a packet of Sweet'N Low into her decaf coffee, attuned to Rachel's needs only moments after re-encountering her.

As they sit together in Monica's apartment, splitting the last Oreo, Ross tells her, "Back in high school, I had a *major* crush on you." (Schwimmer pauses meaningfully before *major,* sucking his tooth and extending his arm like a Supreme, or a running back barreling toward a first down.)

Aniston's response is beautifully understated. She meets Schwimmer's gaze, a smile tickling the edges of her mouth, before replying gently: "I knew."

"I always figured you just thought I was Monica's geeky older brother," Ross responds, surprised.

"I did," says Rachel. (This scene had initially taken place at Ross's apartment, as his friends helped him put together his new IKEA furniture. Rachel would tell him, "Thank you for a wonderful wedding night," as they laughingly snapped the legs onto his new coffee table.)

The scene is tender and awkward and funny, its emotional beats studded by a recurring desire to gently prick any lingering sentiment. "Listen," Ross asks, demonstrating his soon-to-be-familiar circuitous method of speech, "do you think, and try not to let my intense vulnerability become any kind of a factor here, but do you think it would be OK if I asked you out sometime, maybe?" Rachel looks back at him soulfully, replying, "Yeah," before softening into a smile and adding, "maybe."

Ross has been given a go-ahead of sorts but tellingly chooses to sit with it rather than pounce: "OK. OK, maybe I will." Ross looks at his Oreo half rather than at Rachel as he ponders her ambiguous invitation, and after she heads off to bed, he lustily eats his cookie and struts around his sister's apartment, headed toward the door. "Hey, what's with you?" Monica asks. Ross replies, "I just grabbed a spoon."

With this closing flourish, *Six of One* demonstrated its abiding interest not only in the saga of Ross and Rachel, but in the perpetual flurry of transformation that would come to define the show. Its characters were motile, alert to quicksilver changes around them, and searching for self-definition. No sooner would one enormous wave wash over them—divorce, or fleeing marriage—than the next set of questions would emerge. (Originally, the pilot was to end with Ross finding out his ex-wife was pregnant with his baby, but this development wound up being postponed for the second episode.) The pilot craftily pulls both Ross and Rachel out of stultifying existences that we can only too readily imagine, placing them in each other's orbit at precisely the moment they might be most receptive to the possibility of a new manner of existing in the world. The real world sucked, but we were going to love it.

CHAPTER 4

HOW YOU DOIN'?

Preparing for the Premiere

Testing, as Preston Beckman knew, was the crucible in which shows were formed. It was where new series made their way onto the fall schedule, and it was where they got pushed off. Beckman, possessed of a doctorate in sociology from NYU, had become head of scheduling for NBC in 1991, shortly after Littlefield had taken over from Brandon Tartikoff. Among Littlefield's many strengths was an acute awareness of his weaknesses, and he knew scheduling was not his forte. Beckman, who had previously been in the audience research department, and whose skills in after-the-fact analysis as an academic were ideal for the work, was put in place to oversee both day-to-day scheduling and overall planning. Beckman had to make sure that new episodes were ready on time, and that both original episodes and repeats were scheduled effectively. He was also the executive who had to anticipate the needs of the schedule and steer the other departments to develop and support new shows that would match those needs.

In early May, about one hundred people filed into a screening room on the NBC lot to take a first look at the *Six of One* pilot. The audience included representatives from every notable department at NBC, including programming, public relations, marketing, and scheduling, and the mission was a brutal if necessary one. Everyone was here to say precisely what was wrong with the show. Backslapping and plaudits were all well and good for another time, but for today, the mission was to poke holes in *Six of One*, to speak bluntly about what faults could be found with it. And the network's assembled brain trust was not yet pleased with the show.

The overall feeling was that the pilot was a touch too cute, its world too elfin to feel genuine. The characters, too, were overly processed, lacking enough detail to distinguish them, both from each other and from other, past sitcom characters. People were also deeply skeptical about the idea of the show's characters' spending so much time in a coffee shop. A coffee shop was too New York and too downtown for the audience to relate to, they feared. "Don't worry," Bright would later tell NBC. "Everybody will be going to the coffee shop after they see this show." The coffee shop was an attempt to clearly delineate the Generation X trappings of this new show. This was a place where young people would be hanging out, all attempts at integrating Pat the Cop and others of his ilk to the contrary.

An internal memo described the show as "not very entertaining, clever, or original," with particular concerns about Ross, who "generated little sympathy." Audience testing found that viewers over the age of thirty-five especially disliked the show, finding it hard to connect with the characters. And some prominent voices at the network, including Eric Cardinal, the head of program research, simply hated the show.

The process was rough, but the overall message—that *Six of One* had not yet found its groove—was borne out by the later audience testing, which mostly agreed with NBC's critique. It received a "high weak" grade, which neither demolished its chances nor notably increased them. NBC West Coast president Don Ohlmeyer worried that some of the lack of enthusiasm was due to the erotic pursuits of Monica, who was seen sleeping with a stranger on a first date. What would audiences think, Ohlmeyer wondered, about such a libertine young woman, and would they continue wanting to spend time with her after glimpsing her in so compromising a position?

Ohlmeyer had audience members at the research screening fill out a questionnaire about extramarital sex, in an effort to gauge viewers' comfort with such displays. Marta Kauffman was breathing fire out of her nose at Ohlmeyer's presumption and at the obnoxiousness of his questionnaire, which basically asked, she believed, if Monica was A) a whore, B) a slut, or C) easy. Ohlmeyer's sexist query was based on a mistaken assumption that the audience for the show was likely to judge Monica rather than identify with her.

Nonetheless, NBC picked up the show for its fall season on May 13, one week after the pilot was filmed. During the call with the showrunners to let them know the good news, the network requested that the show acquire a new title. The series, they decided, should be called *Friends*. Kevin Bright was unruffled by the request, and said as much: "If you're going to put it on Thursday night, you can call it *Kevorkian*, for all we care!"

The network was confident that a show about six humorous, attractive twentysomethings would play well with youthful audiences, but it had no guarantees that that audience could expand beyond its core. The hope, in the mind of NBC public-relations head Flody Suarez and others, was that people would tune in and note in astonishment, "That's who I was!" or "That's who I am!" or "That's who I will be!"

There was also talk on the NBC lot of more substantive changes to the pilot. The testing suggested that the male characters were viewed as being too similar, which may have reflected the fact that the show featured three brown-haired men. Perhaps the solution, some thought, was to recast one of the starring roles, or to add supporting characters to liven it up.

A concern elaborated by Littlefield and others suggested that there needed to be more of a professional life for the show's characters, establishing existences for the six protagonists outside of their apartments and the coffee shop. But for all of his concerns, Littlefield was also intent on building a network at which passionate voices would be listened to. After strong pushback from NBC's Jamie Tarses and Warner Bros.' David Janollari, both intent on preserving Kauffman and Crane's initial vision, NBC decided, tremulously, to avoid making any major changes to *Friends*—although we did briefly see each of the characters at work in forthcoming episodes.

NBC already knew that it was retooling its Thursday-night lineup around *Seinfeld* and was shifting *Mad About You* over from Wednesdays to join it. The idea of adding a third sitcom about urbane New Yorkers was an appealing one, and Kauffman and Crane's show was tentatively penciled in for the eight thirty slot, between *Mad About You* and *Seinfeld*. Meanwhile, NBC's buzzy new hospital drama, *ER*, with a young, attractive cast of doctors and nurses (including George Clooney and Julianna Margulies) and a raw, handheld aesthetic, was slotted in at ten P.M.

The show the network was most excited about, though, was *Madman of the People*, featuring returning star Dabney Coleman as a cantankerous newspaper columnist displeased to find himself working for his daughter. *Madman of the People* was scheduled for the nine thirty slot on Thursdays, there to coast in the wake of *Seinfeld* and grease the path to the new *ER*. Networks were entrusted with entertaining America, but their sense of what audiences wanted to see was often wildly off base.

With *Mad About You*, on which she had an ongoing guest-starring role, and *Friends* scheduled for the same night, intrepid viewers could watch Lisa Kudrow going back-to-back on different New York–set sitcoms. Crane thought it was so strange that he decided to call *Mad About You* creator Danny Jacobson. What would he think about making Phoebe and Ursula twin sisters? Jacobson agreed, and a rope was extended to lash together one of NBC's current hits with a show they hoped would be the next tent pole of Must-See TV. In retrospect, Crane was unsure whether he would have been so kind in offering a helping hand to a totally untested new show.

Marta Kauffman passed along the pilot script to her husband, musician Michael Skloff, and tasked him with writing a theme for the show. Skloff got in the car to pick up their five-year-old daughter and turned on the car radio. The Beatles' "Paperback Writer" came on the stereo, and John Lennon and Paul McCartney's euphoria captured the precise feeling that Skloff had while reading the script.

In writing the music, Skloff kept his ear trained on the exuberant sound of 1960s pop he had summoned on his FM dial: the Beatles, but also the Monkees and the sunny vocal tones of the early British Invasion. Skloff thought the song should sound like the feeling of waking up on a Saturday morning with a smile on your face.

Skloff was no lyricist, but he decided to pen a rudimentary set of lyrics to accompany his music. The show was about friendship, and being a friend meant being there for other people. He came up with one line he thought was pretty good and could serve as the chorus for his ditty: "I'll be there for you."

Skloff was put to work finding an artist to record the theme song. He was summoned to the producers' office, where his attention was directed to a towering stack of Warner Bros. CDs sitting on a table. After being turned down by R.E.M.'s Michael Stipe and 10,000 Maniacs' Natalie Merchant (who he suggested record as a duo) and They Might Be Giants, Skloff came on a duo that he thought might channel the Lennon/McCartney vibe. They might not have been the household names that Stipe and Merchant, or even They Might Be Giants, were, but what if the Rembrandts were to record the show's theme song?

In the demo, Skloff had used some processed drum sounds to provide a drum fill at one particular moment in the song. After recording with the Rembrandts, he sent the final version to Bright. Almost immediately, the phone rang. "Where's that drum fill?" Bright asked. "Well," responded Skloff, "we have real drums now, so the drummer just did what felt natural in that moment."

Unbeknownst to Skloff, Bright had gone ahead and begun editing together a credit sequence, and had used the four beats of the drum fill to make four fast visual cuts. Without that fill, Bright's video didn't quite work. Skloff was sent back to the studio to record some new drum hits. He was brainstorming with the engineer for the session, Kerry Butler, and someone suggested filling the musical space with a series of hand claps. There were no better ideas, so Skloff, along with two of the show's assistants, got behind a microphone and clapped along with the song. The most memorable sequence of one of the most memorable television theme songs ever had just been recorded.

With the show given the green light to air, Kauffman and Crane's next task was to hire a writing staff. Kauffman and Crane wanted writers who were hungry, who had not yet been formed by their experience on other shows. The inspiration for *Friends* had come from Kauffman's and Crane's own time as struggling writers in their twenties living in Manhattan, but they were in their midthirties now. They were more than a decade older than their characters, and their twentysomething experiences, which were still so vibrant in their minds, were also a decade out of date.

Kauffman's and Crane's desks were piled high with books and magazines and article clippings about the lives of Generation X. They wanted to understand all the nuances of youth culture, from the music to the clothing to the pop culture references to the preferred hangouts. The questions underlying their search were fairly simple: What was it like to be twenty-five years old in 1994? How did young college graduates speak, banter, and think right now?

To help answer those questions, Kauffman and Crane decided that they needed a young writing staff. They wanted to be able to draw on the experiences of their writers to put the show together, both in mining their lives for story ideas and in serving as all-purpose bullshit detectors for its creators.

Adam Chase had grown accustomed to the sound of a grown woman screaming at him by the time he was twenty-two. He and his Northwestern University classmate Ira Ungerleider had moved out to Los Angeles after graduation in the hopes of pursuing careers in television. Chase wound up with a job as an assistant to an agent who enjoyed shouting and throwing office equipment to express her frustration. This was just the nature of Hollywood, Chase thought, and he grimly stuck it out until he could find the next gig.

Like practically every other sentient college graduate with dreams of writing comedy, Chase aspired to one day make the staff of *The Simpsons*. The goal, for now, was to get a production-assistant job at Gracie Films, which produced the show, and Chase peppered Gracie's offices with letters and phone messages. One day, he called and happened to get a live person on the other end, who had thought Chase was a producer calling. Chase made them laugh, and they told him that they actually were looking for a PA and hired him.

It was a dream job, made even better by the opportunity to work in close proximity to James L. Brooks. Brooks, who had been responsible for *The Mary Tyler Moore Show* and *Taxi*, among others, was generous in offering his time to aspiring writers. Chase and Ungerleider sweated through writing a spec script (an unassigned script for an already-existing show, intended to serve as a calling card for an emerging writer) for *Seinfeld* that they planned to show Brooks. After tossing a first attempt, Chase and Ungerleider polished a second attempt a dozen times, and then when they had something they were pleased with, they brazenly stamped "first draft" on the cover and submitted it to Brooks's colleague Richard Sakai. Sakai liked their script and passed it along to Brooks, who offered them an opportunity to write one script for a show called *Phenom*.

Chase and Ungerleider eventually made the staff, and when the show was canceled at the end of the season, they were juggling offers from a number of shows. They had strong interest from the producers of the onetime ABC hit *Grace Under Fire*; they could sign on for the Dudley Moore–starring *Daddy's Girls*, or they could write for the variety series *The Martin Short Show*. Both writers admired Short, a big star and a genuinely nice man who managed to remember the names of lowly writers like themselves when he stopped by the *Phenom* set. Chase and Ungerleider helped polish the *Martin Short* pilot and felt like their choice was made for them. The show would undoubtedly be a hit, and they would get to work with a comedic icon.

Then they got called for an interview for a new show by David Crane and Marta Kauffman and had the chance to look at the show's pilot. Chase and Ungerleider were thunderstruck by the echoes of their own lives. Here were characters who sounded just like them. Chase and Ungerleider had emerged from the same bookish East Coast Jewish milieu as Kauffman and Crane. Chase knew he could instantly summon that overly caffeinated, verbose, linguistically tricky voice.

Moreover, the life the show was describing was one Chase and Ungerleider had lived. When they first moved to Los Angeles, they had lived in a cramped three-bedroom in West Hollywood with three other people, including Andrew Reich, who would be brought onto *Friends'* writing staff for the fourth season. Chase felt like Kauffman and Crane's pilot inadvertently channeled his own life, with friends in the bedroom next door and others down the hall. Chase and Ungerleider took the *Friends* job.

Mike Sikowitz had been working in advertising in New York, where one of his clients was ABC. The network regularly sent over advance copies of scripts for Sikowitz and his fellow entry-level writers of ad copy to look over. After reading the scripts, they were tasked with writing short blurbs about new episodes for the likes of *TV Guide* or *People*, or brief advertisements that might run on radio stations. Sikowitz had been plugging away at these for some time when he had a realization: The people writing these scripts were likely having a whole lot more fun than he was, and making more money to boot.

He called his writing partner Jeff Astrof, then working in finance, and suggested they try their hand at some spec scripts. In the early 1990s, sitcoms were still booming, and the television industry had a seemingly endless need for young writers to staff the dozens of comedy series then on the air. "Let's take a look at these," Sikowitz told Astrof. "Maybe we could write one."

The two young writers set to work laying out a spec script of *Seinfeld*. In it, George went to get his pants tailored, while Jerry was embroiled in a cheating scandal in an adult-education class. On the basis of their spec, and a connection with an agent, Sikowitz and Astrof decided to move out to Los Angeles, where they found work writing for *Hangin' with Mr. Cooper* and the animated series *Duckman*.

They were used to the process of auditioning for new series, which Sikowitz called dog-and-pony shows. They would be summoned, trot out all their best tricks, and then go home to pant by the phone for a treat that might not ever come. So when a call came in for a new show by Marta Kauffman and David Crane, they were unruffled. After watching the pilot, they were impressed with what they had seen. The creators were clearly talented writers, and meeting them in person, they felt genuine and like just the kind of people they would want to work for.

Alexa Junge had been so low on the writers' totem pole that she was not allowed to go upstairs at William Morris to visit her agent. Her agent had taken on Junge as a client before joining the firm, and William Morris had told her in no uncertain terms to drop Junge. Instead, they would meet in the building's lobby, where she would smuggle Junge a pile of photocopied pilot scripts to pore over.

In the spring of 1994, Junge headed out to a shabby inn in Palm Springs to read this year's haul, and stopped at the names of David Crane and Marta Kauffman. Junge had also been part of the New York theater scene and had seen their shows *Personal* and *A . . . My Name Is Alice*. Junge had been working for Nickelodeon and was struggling to connect with network series, but she had really enjoyed the script for Kauffman and Crane's *Family Album* the year prior. In the margins of the script for *Friends*, Junge scribbled her calorie count for the day alongside copious notes.

She asked her agent to submit a play she had written as her writing sample for the new show, and her agent refused. They had submitted the same material last year for *Family Album*, when she had not been hired. Junge pleaded, arguing that Kauffman and Crane likely had not even had a chance to read her play. She won her argument, with her agent offering to say it was her mistake if anyone noticed. Kauffman and Crane called days later, wanting to meet. Hers was a voice they were looking for, especially given the overwhelmingly male staff they had assembled. She brought her food-stained script into her meeting to show Kauffman and Crane one note she had jotted down right near the calorie count: "This is so special."

The new writing staff, which also included Jeff Greenstein and Jeff Strauss, who were content to take the downward step from showrunners to writers to move to network television and collaborate with Kauffman and Crane again, was tasked with the job of planning for the season to come. Kauffman and Crane had a rough sense of where the story should go, and a few plot ideas, but little more. They knew that Ross's ex-wife, Carol, would be pregnant, and that the first season would track her pregnancy. Kauffman felt strongly that the season would culminate in Carol's giving birth. They also knew that Ross and Rachel's relationship would develop in some fashion, although precisely how far along they would get remained to be determined.

Beyond that, there were a handful of semideveloped stories. They knew that one episode would revolve around a sonogram for Carol, who would be pregnant with Ross's baby. There was the idea of having Joey serve as a butt double for Al Pacino. They even knew that Ross and Rachel would eventually have sex at his museum—a plot point that would not emerge until the second season. The rest was left to unfold in the writers' room.

Greenstein remembered that when he had worked on *Dream On*, he had devoted time—too much of it—to coming up with a pithy title for each episode. The title would appear on the screen at the beginning of an episode, and Greenstein, along with Kauffman and Crane, wanted the titles to properly set a mood before the episode started. In planning for *Friends*, it was understood that the episode titles were unlikely to ever appear onscreen, but Crane and Kauffman were cognizant that fans might come across them in *TV Guide* or the listings of their daily newspaper. They talked it over and realized that even die-hard fans were unlikely to remember the name of a given episode when talking it over in homeroom or a nearby cubicle the next day. Instead, it would be, "Hey, did you see the one with the . . . ?" Since fans were already going to refer to episodes that way, why not simply make that the formula for the actual titles as well? *Friends'* episode titling was born, with nearly every episode's name beginning "The One with" or "The One Where." (Even the ones that diverged did so only partially, like "The One Hundredth.")

At Kauffman and Crane's urging, much of what the writers brought was material from their own lives. Jeff Greenstein remembered working a temp job at a Japanese insurance company as a claims processor soon after moving to Los Angeles. Everyone was obsessing over the crunching of numbers whose purpose Greenstein only dimly understood. The mixture of intense seriousness and ludicrousness of purpose activated Greenstein's comic taste buds; he recognized the Kafkaesque undertones of his workplace.

After six months, Greenstein's superiors wanted to give him a promotion to a full-time position. Instead of being pleased, Greenstein panicked. He was not a claims processor, nor did he ever want to be one, and the idea of progressing in a career that was anathema to his ambitions horrified him. Instead of accepting the promotion, he summarily quit. Greenstein's risky career decision wound up becoming Chandler's, who would also quit a mysterious data-processing job in search of more meaningful employment.

Originally, the pilot had gone into more depth on Chandler's professional life, with Rachel coming to his office to work on her résumé. Those scenes had been cut, but *Friends* retained an initial interest in Chandler's professional dilemmas, having him take a professional-aptitude test that suggested he was best qualified to—of course—process numbers. It was like a fever dream of Greenstein's transposed onto one of *Friends*' characters, retaining that similar sensation of twentysomething aimlessness.

Writers also drew on the experiences of their friends and colleagues for inspiration. During the first season, planning commenced on a Thanksgiving episode, soon to become a tradition on the show. Greenstein and Strauss suggested that one of the characters should be an outspoken Thanksgiving pessimist. The sardonic Chandler was the best fit for the role, but they lacked the backstory that would justify his grinchiness. Finally, Greenstein turned to Jeff Strauss and said, "Well, we could do your story."

Greenstein and Strauss had been classmates at Tufts, where they began their writing partnership, and Thanksgiving of sophomore year, Greenstein decided he did not feel up to going home for the holiday. His mother had died the previous summer, and home felt like an uncertain place. He asked Strauss if he could spend Thanksgiving with his family, which sounded like a respite from the crisis at home.

That weekend, Strauss's parents decided to announce that they were getting divorced. Greenstein was uncomfortably present as Strauss and his sister wrestled with the changes coming to their family. It was, of course, a perfect plotline for Chandler, and an explanation of sorts for his use of sarcasm as a shield deflecting the world's arrows.

The actors had varying amounts of sitcom experience, but it was James Burrows who understood the material, and the form, best and could offer necessary guidance. In an early run-through, Matthew Perry came up with a small bit of business that won a laugh, delivering a funny look after speaking his line. Perry returned to the gesture later on, garnering another laugh. Burrows interrupted the rehearsal and approached Perry. "I just want to tell you you shouldn't do that after the line," Burrows told him. "Because if this show is a success, which I think it will be, that will be all you're known for."

Burrows knew how television could chew up gifted actors and turn them overnight into caricatures known for a single tic. The small gesture you created as a charming button to a scene could become, a few years down the road, the only thing anyone ever asked you to do. It was better not to take that laugh.

Kauffman observed her actors and noticed that the show's male actors were more willing to pitch ideas than the women. If they thought a particular joke wasn't clicking, they would mess around and make each other laugh until they had something they preferred. Kauffman believed that the female performers were still fearful of embracing their inner comedians—something that would change as the series went on.

Burrows's presence encouraged the young actors to think of their costars as their colleagues, not their competitors. He was intent on *Friends'* not becoming one of those shows where actors counted their lines and complained when they lagged behind. This was a show where an injury to one was an injury to all, and everyone's success rode on collective achievement.

The director offered the use of his lavish private dressing room for the cast to hang out in together between takes. They would gather in there and play poker, giving them a chance to banter and enjoy themselves away from the cameras.

While filming the second episode, before the show's premiere, Jane Sibbett, who had been cast as Carol after the original performer, Anita Barone, had demanded a larger role, walked around a corner and came on the three female stars of *Friends*. It was raining, and there they were, jumping in a puddle and splashing each other gleefully. Sibbett felt like she was privy to a privileged moment. If Aniston, Cox, and Kudrow could play like good friends when no one else was watching, it was just possible that they might be able to convey that sense of comradeship to the vast television audience.

After the cast had filmed a handful of episodes, but before the show premiered, Burrows called Les Moonves to ask for a favor. Might he borrow the Warner Bros. jet to take the *Friends* cast to Las Vegas? Burrows wanted to give the cast a well-deserved break, but he also was looking out for the show. He believed that a crucial part of his work was to encourage the natural camaraderie that was blossoming between them. Burrows hoped that their respect for each other could turn into genuine love and affection, and that those feelings would be visible in their work together.

Moonves agreed, and the seven of them flew to Nevada. Burrows took them out to dinner at Wolfgang Puck's restaurant at Caesars Palace, and as they dug into their entrees, Burrows told them that this would be their last shot at anonymity. The actors looked at him, confused, and Burrows explained that after *Friends* premiered, they would not be able to enter a restaurant or casino without being mobbed. "You're kidding me," they told Burrows, not yet ready to accept what the future held in store for them.

The actors were interested in gambling after dinner but didn't have enough money to cut loose and enjoy themselves. Burrows took out his checkbook and wrote out a check to each of them. Burrows's only regret, later on, was that he didn't save the check stubs. What better memento could there have been of this pregnant moment in the history of American television?

Littlefield's intuition about an audience's hungering to see themselves onscreen was borne out by the earliest responses to the show. After being hired, Jeff Strauss flew with his wife to Northern California to visit her sister. *Friends* had not even premiered yet, but promos for the show were starting to run on NBC. On the airplane, Strauss's wife had begun chatting with her seatmate, and they exchanged notes about their professional lives. She mentioned her husband's writing for *Friends,* and the woman on the airplane told her, "I think that's going to be my new favorite show." Strauss and his wife never saw the woman from the airplane again, but she was a reminder that there was a whole audience of young television viewers who thought *Friends* might be their favorite new show, before even seeing it.

PART II

. . .

MUST-SEE TV

(Seasons 1 through 3)

CHAPTER 5

GUM WOULD BE PERFECTION

The First Season Debuts

"Oh, no, you might well moan," reviewer John J. O'Connor wrote in *The New York Times* on September 29, 1994, "not another group of pals sitting around whining and nursing their anxieties, getting up once in a while to test the passing Zeitgeist." *Entertainment Weekly*'s Ken Tucker also began his review with a note of caution regarding *Friends*' familiarity: "If I tell you that it's a show about a bunch of attractive yuppies sitting around talking, what do you think of? *thirtysomething, Seinfeld, Mad About You,* yadda-yadda-yadda." But the show surprised Tucker with its comic vigor: "At its best, *Friends* operates like a first-rate Broadway farce, complete with slamming doors, twisty plots, and intricately strung together jokes. And even when it's not at its best, the crack acting and piquant punch lines give *Friends* a momentum and charm that win you over even if you're not laughing."

Tucker offered effusive praise to both the writers and the cast. "Kauffman and Crane can take an utterly standard sitcom scene—a discussion among the chums about whether foreplay is more important to women than to men—and turn it into a tensely funny playlet with a beginning, middle, and end, all before the opening credits." Tucker singled out each member of the cast for praise, calling Kudrow "a cross between Goldie Hawn and Teri Garr [who, unbeknownst to Tucker, would later play Phoebe's mother on the show] with, I dunno, substance," and referring to LeBlanc as "a rarity—a hunk with a gift for deadpan comedy." Tucker went on to praise Cox for having "the most prominent, um, biceps—yeah, that's the ticket, *biceps*—in prime time," about which the less said, the better.

After his initial burst of dyspepsia, O'Connor was also enthusiastic about the debut of *Friends,* comparing it to *Dream On* and saying that it "promises to be equally offbeat and seductive." "The cast is appealing," O'Connor concludes, "the dialogue is pitch-perfect 1994, the time-slot is between the solidly established *Mad About You* at 8 P.M. and *Seinfeld* at 9 P.M. *Friends* comes as close as a new series can get to having everything."

There was generalized agreement that *Friends* was privileged enough to have been born standing on third base. "Wedged happily between *Mad About You* and *Seinfeld,*" wrote the *Chicago Tribune*'s Ken Parish Perkins, "this comedy series from the producers of HBO's *Dream On* would have to be an utter disaster—which it isn't—not to finish as the season's highest-rated new comedy."

Howard Rosenberg of the *Los Angeles Times* was the most enthusiastic of the early reviewers, calling *Friends* "flat-out the best comedy series of the new season." After describing the premise, he noted, "It sounds vacuous, and it is, sort of, but wittily vacuous, with crisply written dialogue adroitly executed by the show's strong ensemble cast." "It's all so light and frothy," Rosenberg concludes, "that after each episode you may be hard-pressed to recall precisely what went on, except that you laughed a lot."

Other reviewers were turned off by what they saw as *Friends'* childishness and lack of comic vigor. NBC's other shows were being wielded as cudgels against *Friends*. "Where *Seinfeld* is smart and appealingly free-form, *Friends* is inane and gimmicky," observed *Time* magazine, who called the show "sophomoric." "This half-hour is completely lacking in charm or intelligence," groused the *Hartford Courant's* James Endrst. He described it as "anemic and unworthy of its Thursday-night time slot."

Numerous critics agreed that *Friends* had a notable burden in introducing so many characters simultaneously. "Producers Marta Kauffman and David Crane are trying to give us enough information to make us care about all six people, in 22 minutes," said *The Baltimore Sun's* David Zurawik. "There's something almost abstract about *Friends,*" noted *Entertainment Weekly's* Tucker. "Even after a few weeks, I'm still not clear about where each of the characters lives and what relationships they have with one another."

Tucker was concerned about how long it had taken him to grasp that Ross was Monica's brother and not her boyfriend, offering some advice to the actors to clear up any unwanted ambiguities: "I'd suggest to [David] Schwimmer that he resist the thoroughly understandable temptation to hug Cox in quite so passionate a manner."

Tom Shales of *The Washington Post* seemed to feel a particular revulsion toward the show, not only panning it as a "ghastly creation" but singling out Kauffman and Crane for abuse. They were "professional panderers" and "the witless duo who do *Dream On* for HBO." The show "comes across like a 30-minute commercial for Dockers or Ikea or light beer, except it's smuttier. . . . You keep waiting for Sally Jessy or some other cluck to interrupt the jabbering. The show is so bad that Sally Jessy would actually come as a relief."

———

When Don Ohlmeyer saw *Friends'* title sequence, after the first episode was broadcast, he was furious. He called Kevin Bright the next day with a pointed question: "What is that title sequence?"

"What do you mean?" Bright asked.

"It's awful. It's terrible," Ohlmeyer blustered. Bright still didn't know what Ohlmeyer was referring to, and asked him to explain his frustration. "It says to the audience, 'We're young, we're hip, we're dancing in a fountain and you can't dance with us.'"

"You really think it says all that?" replied Bright. Ohlmeyer was insistent that the sequence, in which the show's six stars fussed with umbrellas and splashed in a fountain, would cause the audience to feel left out, and demanded that Bright reinstate the original title sequence, set to R.E.M.'s "Shiny Happy People," which had run before the presentation of the pilot.

Bright's initial impulse was to fight, but on second consideration, he called back Ohlmeyer and offered a compromise. What if they worked up a new title sequence that was half Bright's and half Ohlmeyer's? "Let me see what it looks like," responded Ohlmeyer. In time for the second episode, Bright put together a new title sequence that mixed clips from the show, much like the "Shiny Happy People" sequence, with the fountain footage. The hybrid version could serve as an under-the-radar refresher in recent developments on the show, being updated every few episodes. In the end, Bright was happy that Ohlmeyer had made such a stink. It was, he believed, one of the only positive contributions Don Ohlmeyer had made to *Friends*.

The first season was a mostly steady, occasionally halting process of discovering what motivated the show's characters. While Ross and Rachel had been ably and efficiently thrust into their own orbits, other characters remained more mysterious to the *Friends* writers. Joey began life as a leather-jacketed lothario with an outer-boroughs affect and an overflowing little black book of conquests. Testing done after the pilot revealed that audiences found Joey off-putting and more than a little familiar, a Tony Danza–style stereotype.

The writers took another look at Joey in the hopes of making him more appealing. He was still a ladies' man, they thought, still someone who preferred a one-night stand to a committed relationship. But now he was more of a guy with a code. The show did not entirely approve of his cocksmanship, although it did regularly laugh off his excesses. But he was now a simpler soul, as writer Jeff Greenstein thought, a kid in a candy store who could not help glutting himself on every possible variety of sweet. Joey was an older brother to the three girls, his urges held in place by the warmth of his affections. And the leather jacket was ditched.

Monica, too, was a mystery. She was supposed to be a den mother for her brother and their wacky friends, with a healing word for every wound and a bandage for every scrape. But that now felt like too limiting a role, with not enough to do when the other characters were caught up in their own romantic pursuits. The writers privately called Monica "the Riddler," because all she seemed to do, in the early episodes, was ask the other characters questions and set up their jokes. Courteney Cox was doing fine work in the role, so it was not a matter of the acting. Instead, it was that Monica herself was a kind of riddle, lacking a central core that future plotlines could be built around.

Kauffman, herself warm and nurturing, had based Monica at least partially on herself but was troubled by the lack of clarity regarding Monica's motivations. She called a meeting and asked writers to come up with a list of adjectives that might describe Monica. Mike Sikowitz raised his hand and offered, "She's inquisitive?"

It took until "The One Where Underdog Gets Away," the show's ninth episode, to glimpse a path forward. The plot had Monica preparing Thanksgiving dinner to everyone's overly demanding specifications. Monica was channeling writer Jeff Strauss's relationship with Thanksgiving.

Strauss had planned and cooked his own Thanksgiving dinner since college, inviting friends to share the holiday with him. He was, in his own estimation, simultaneously obsessively solicitous and terribly demanding. He was the guy who told all his friends exactly where, when, and how they would be celebrating Thanksgiving, while also cooking potatoes five different ways to satisfy his picky friends. Like Strauss, Monica was trying to control everyone around her while also fruitlessly seeking to meet everyone's needs.

Adam Chase and one or two other writers were hanging out on the set, and they noticed Courteney Cox straightening the furniture in her pretend apartment after everyone else had left. She was playing with something hidden between the lines of the script, something inherent to her character that had not yet been fully teased out. Monica was freaking out over invisible dust motes, and Chase realized that they had stumbled into a breakthrough.

They brought their accidental discovery back to the writers' room, and Monica, who had previously been opaque as a character, became substantially clearer. The idea of concentrating on Monica and Rachel as roommates, and playing up Rachel's slovenliness against Monica's rage for order, gave Monica's character colors she had previously lacked. Alexa Junge saw it as an ideal opportunity to unleash all of her type-A personality traits and share them with Monica.

And the new take on Monica as an obsessive-compulsive neat freak illuminated a path forward for the character that allowed the writers to move her away from her Riddler status. The idea that Monica had OCD-like tendencies opened up dozens of potential story lines that had previously remained hidden to the writers.

The OCD was a fictional addition, but there was a part of Cox that wanted to take care of her friends, that wanted to guide them to the right decisions. Cox was the one who went around the set telling everyone precisely what model of car phone to purchase. Cox was the one who knew how long it might take to rehearse a scene or for one of her costars to go through makeup. She was the one who could sketch a minute-by-minute plan for the next day's work, factoring in every detail of her five costars' schedules. Cox would clean up her costars' dressing rooms when they got too messy. Monica was not Courteney Cox, but there were elements of Cox's personality that were heightened and exaggerated for the purposes of creating Monica.

The pilot had featured only Monica's apartment, along with a glimpse of Ross's new place. But by the second episode, Kauffman and Crane knew they needed a place for the boys to live as well. The hallway set would come in handy now, as Chandler and Joey were to live directly across the hall. Production designer John Shaffner and set decorator

Greg Grande would need to build and furnish a second apartment. The boys' apartment would have to be smaller, darker, shabbier, and less attractively decorated.

Grande wanted the boys' apartment to flaunt Chandler and Joey's execrable taste. Grande found the ugliest couch he could and then matched it with a workout bench (standard-issue overgrown-adolescent ornamentation) and a pair of unfortunate stools. For Grande, the pièce de résistance was the beige-and-brown cut-pile carpet draped across the floor, which looked like it had suffered a series of catastrophic spills from which it had never been able to recover. Who in their right mind, Grande wondered, would keep such an ugly thing?

Scenes from early episodes had taken place in Chandler's white-collar workplace and in Monica's restaurant, but Kauffman and Crane soon realized that audience interest plummeted as soon as *Friends* followed its characters to work. (This would change some in later seasons, as the show got craftier about its uses of the workplace.) The writers were intent on demonstrating their lives outside of Central Perk, but audiences truly did not want to depart the charmed inner circle. Eventually, the writers came up with a solution. Instead of venturing out, *Friends* would bring its adventures back home, with its characters recounting the tales of what had transpired elsewhere. This would be a show in which stories were often retold instead of depicted.

The workplace would recede into the background on *Friends*, only occasionally glimpsed. Ross had his job at the Museum of Prehistoric History, and later a gig as a professor of paleontology; Phoebe worked as a masseuse; Monica went from an assistant chef to having a kitchen of her own; Joey went out for auditions and won a role on the soap opera *Days of Our Lives* as egotistical doctor Drake Ramoray; Chandler would quit his job to avoid having to worry over the WENUS, the Weekly Estimated Net Usage Systems. (We would see a bit more of the work life of Rachel, whose flourishing career was a key aspect of her character.) There was a shared aura of professional floundering, with Monica losing her job, Joey's agent suggesting gay porn, and Chandler later desperate for an internship at an advertising firm where he would be a decade older than his colleagues.

Ross, who has somehow managed to complete a doctorate by the time we first meet him, is treated like a walking punch line, his scientific bent proof positive, for his friends, of his irredeemable geekiness. *Friends* knows it can only occasionally rouse itself to express any interest in its characters' professional lives and chooses to make light of it. When everyone at Central Perk offers suggestions about why their bosses seem to hate them, Joey takes umbrage: "Or *maybe* it's because you're all hanging around here at eleven thirty on a Wednesday!"

The cast would get together on Thursday evenings each week to watch the latest episode of the show together as it aired. They would use the opportunity to exchange notes about how to improve the show, and even about each other's performances. At the very start of their time together, Courteney Cox had asked her costars to give her any notes they might have about her performance, and the weekly watch parties extended the custom, giving the actors a place and time of their own to discuss what they wanted to see from the show.

Ross and Rachel's burgeoning relationship was the driver of much of the building enthusiasm for *Friends*. And the slow-burn technique, in which romance was forever being delayed, was incredibly effective at creating momentum for the show. The strategy was clearly descended from that of *Friends'* Must-See TV predecessor *Cheers*, which had Ted Danson's lusty bartender Sam and Shelley Long's intellectual barmaid Diane push and pull at each other for five full seasons. *Cheers* had proved that willthey-or-won't-they could be a highly effective sitcom strategy, wielding romance and emotion as a counterweight to comedy, and using its ebb and flow to keep viewers tuning in consistently, week after week.

The show allows us to stand a half step ahead of its characters. As the first season progressed, audiences watched Ross and Rachel smile at each other, listened to the soft tones of their polite conversations, sensed something brewing between them, even as Ross was crippled by post-divorce doubt and Rachel was struggling to catch up with the working world she had hoped to bypass entirely.

Ross moped through much of the first season, the loss of Carol still stinging, and the notion of having lost her to a woman the lingering humiliation that he cannot forget. Rachel shook him out of his self-absorption, her presence luring him back to the world. In "The One with the Sonogram at the End," the first episode after the pilot, Ross looked over Rachel's shoulder, moaning in combined pleasure and agony, when she asked him, "Didn't you think you were just going to meet someone, fall in love, and that would be it?"

"The One with the East German Laundry Detergent" (season 1, episode 5) brought the two characters together in quasi-romantic circumstances for the first time since the pilot, for an activity that Ross saw as a date and Rachel treated as laundry day. Rachel, new to the world outside suburban Long Island, admits to being a "laundry virgin." Ross, rising to the occasion with a clever double entendre, tells her, "Don't worry, I'll use the gentle cycle." At the end of the episode, Ross steps up to save Rachel's cart from a pushy interloper, and Rachel unexpectedly kisses him out of gratitude. Ross takes a step back, fondles a pile of sheets, and then walks directly into an open dryer door.

We are jolted out of what we come to believe is our private secret, shared only with Ross, in "The One with the Blackout," when after Ross argues that passion burns out, replaced by trust and security, Ross tells Rachel, "I see a big passion in your future." We can practically see Ross's mental gears turning frenziedly as he parses Rachel's reply of "You're so great"; until Joey, flopped sidelong in a chair, breaks the spell: "It's *never* gonna happen." Joey goes on to explain that Ross has spent too much time in "the friend zone" (a now-familiar, somewhat sexist relationship concept first introduced here) to escape it now: "You're mayor of the zone." "Blackout," which was supposed to be part of a network-wide themed block of episodes (only *Seinfeld* chose not to make use of the blackout) and featured Chandler trapped in an ATM vestibule with Victoria's Secret model Jill Goodacre, felt to the writing staff like the first episode that got an audience buzzing about *Friends*.

Ross is a wounded teddy bear, pining for an unattainable crush, but there are darker hints of a less likable version of Ross to come. After Rachel meets Italian hunk Paolo (Cosimo Fusco), Ross pulls him aside to tell him that he and Rachel are "kind of a thing," saying, "Rachel and I should be together." There is something creepy about Ross's blatant interference in Rachel's romantic life and in his blithe assumption that he knows what Rachel wants, in the complete absence of any such assurances from the woman he yearns for. Audiences loved Ross, the show's first breakout character, but there were intimations here already of what later audiences would find so off-putting about him. Ross was a romantic, but he was also a particular kind of romantic who believed his emotions conveyed a sense of ownership of his beloved.

For Kudrow, the first season was full of "pinch me" moments, where she realized that all the career struggle that had preceded this moment had led her to this privileged place. Kudrow kept pulling the producers to the side in down moments with a single question: "Are the ratings good enough?" She wanted to know if *Friends* was long for this world, or if she would be back to hustling for auditions come next pilot season.

The first genuine test of the show's lasting power would be the "back nine." New series were often green-lit for an initial run of thirteen episodes. This allowed the networks an opportunity to reassess a show's development midway through the season—and to avoid throwing an entire season's worth of money after a disaster. To be picked up for the back nine was to receive a full twenty-two-episode order, rounding out a complete season of the show.

The ratings indicated that *Friends* was adeptly finding an audience a handful of episodes in, so property master Marjorie Coster-Praytor was shocked when, one morning, Crane and Kauffman summoned the cast and the crew to the stage and announced that they had bad news and good news. "The bad news," Kauffman told them, "is that we did not get picked up for the back nine." A ripple of shock spread through the gathered crowd. Everyone felt that they had done good work on *Friends.* How could it be that they weren't being picked up? Kauffman let the news sink in for a long moment before carrying on: "The good news is we got picked up for eleven."

Cast members were crying with joy at the powerful vote of confidence from NBC, which was only further emphasized when they arrived at work the next morning to find none other than NBC president Warren Littlefield, clad in an apron, serving omelets to the *Friends* team.

For the remainder of the first season, Ross's friends would watch him silently pine for Rachel alongside the audience and provide a stream of acerbic commentary on his longing. Chandler spies on Ross watching Rachel bend over to pour coffee at her new job at Central Perk at the start of "The One with All the Poker" and swiftly bursts his bubble of soulful yearning: "Could you *want* her more?"

Chandler's quip was a reminder that *Friends* created its own language and its own conversational styles. The "Could you . . ." setup, conjoined with Perry's placing the accent on the unexpected *want,* became Chandler's instantly recognizable verbal tic. The writers soon learned never to italicize any word of Chandler's dialogue, as Perry would inevitably select an entirely different word to emphasize. Joey became famous for his three-word come-on, usually delivered as his eyes lavishly caressed a woman's body: "How *you* doin'?" Ross would wind his way with exaggerated slowness through a line, stopping to interrupt his thought, raise an eyebrow, or pause significantly. Perhaps this was what Burrows had warned the cast about when steering them away from catchphrases, but Perry in particular managed to use his off-kilter verbal rhythms to surprise audiences nonetheless.

Of all the first-season episodes, "Poker" is perhaps the most emotionally resonant, with Ross and Rachel sparring for an audience of their friends during a male vs. female poker game. The script, inspired by the poker games in Burrows's dressing room, expertly toggles between the manufactured drama of the poker table and Rachel's anxious wait for news about a potential job offer. Ross, his masculine braggadocio always a paper-thin membrane covering a deep well of insecurity, crows that he will not be taking it easy on Rachel once the cards are dealt. When the game is interrupted by a call for Rachel, informing her that she did not get the job, Ross's desire to flirtatiously squabble instantly evaporates.

Ross ultimately folds, the camera zooming in on his face as he calmly admits defeat: "When you don't have the cards, you don't have the cards." He then directs Chandler's and Joey's attention to Rachel on the other side of the table, pointing at her and telling them, "But look how happy she is." The three guys look at each other for a long beat, then everyone dives for Ross's cards.

The first season of *Friends* encourages us to follow along behind Ross as his feelings for Rachel grow, and as his seeming incompetence at acting on those feelings also balloons. Rachel keeps taunting Ross with descriptions of her dream man. Rachel is looking for a man who could be "your best friend, but can also make your toes curl." Ross hopes to be just that, even as his sense of his own desirability has been badly wounded by Carol's leaving him for a woman.

Kauffman had entered the inaugural season working on the assumption that *Friends* would wrap up for the year with the birth of Ross and Carol's baby. It was left to Burrows to approach her and gently share the widely held opinion that no one cared about Ross's baby. The show pivoted on Ross and Rachel, and the conclusion of the season had to revolve around their relationship. The birth of Ben was bumped to the penultimate episode of the first season, "The One with the Birth," and the final episode was devoted to Ross and Rachel's fitful romance.

There was a fear among the writers that they were in danger of painting themselves into a corner, with Ross endlessly pining and Rachel forever oblivious, unless they began to advance the plot. There had been talk in the writers' room of having Ross impulsively kiss Rachel when their car hits a bump on a road trip, and then having an extended discussion of what it meant that they had just kissed. The idea was to evoke memories of Woody Allen and Diane Keaton in *Annie Hall,* and writer Jeff Greenstein spoke up: "Guys, I don't know if I want to see that scene." Greenstein was unsure if Ross and Rachel were like Allen and Keaton, and told his colleagues he was not excited about the proposed conversation.

Crane asked Greenstein what he might prefer instead, and his thoughts turned to the work of Jane Austen. Greenstein's wife had written her senior thesis at UC Berkeley on Austen, and when they had gotten together, he had read all of Austen's novels. "You know," he told the room, "if Jane Austen were writing this story it would go like this: It would be Ross is being called away on some business thing, a paleontological dig or something, and he's gonna miss Rachel's birthday, so he leaves behind some small gift for her, something really specific and personal and beautiful that speaks to the depths of his feelings [for] her. He leaves it behind, he goes on this trip, and Rachel gets the gift, it's so beautiful that she starts to fall in love with him. By the time Ross is scheduled to get back, Rachel can't wait to see him because she finally wants to tell him how much she cares for him, and he gets off the plane with another girl." After a beat, Crane said, "Well, let's do that!" But there were still days of arguments in the writers' room over the finale, even after Greenstein's fix.

At the start of "The One Where Rachel Finds Out," Rachel is immensely touched by Ross's purchasing a beautiful brooch that she admired in a store window some months prior. Chandler unthinkingly takes the bait, offhandedly commenting that Ross has always been partial to bold romantic gestures: "Remember back in college, when he fell in love with Carol and bought her that ridiculously expensive crystal duck?" Director Kevin Bright cuts to Joey looking over at Chandler in near-panic, shifting away from him toward the edge of the couch. "What did you just say?" Rachel demands. Chandler, his chest heaving, clears his throat before responding: "Crystal duck."

The season ends with Rachel, having rushed to the airport to confront Ross, smelling the flowers she has brought for him while waiting for Ross to emerge, an expectant smile teasing across her face. Aniston is remarkable here, her emotional openness heartrending. We know already that her heart is to be broken, with Ross shown kissing an unfamiliar new woman as they both exit the plane, but she doesn't know it yet, and her optimism that love will treat her more gently this time is surprisingly moving.

The first-season cliffhanger, then, is actually less of a cliffhanger than a deliberate withholding of an emotional resolution. We know that Ross and Rachel are going to suffer from a legendarily terrible case of poor timing, and our hearts ache for Rachel, who has finally caught up to Ross just as he vanishes into another relationship.

The first season of *Friends* was that rarest of things in mid-1990s television: a fully formed story with an emotionally satisfying romantic arc and a conclusion that left viewers hungering for more. None of these had been invented by *Friends*—the 1980s drama-comedy hybrid *Moonlighting* had also artfully worked the ebbs and flows of its central relationship—but few of its comedy compatriots sought to craft a story that viewers could return to for laughs and emotional sustenance.

If you watched the first season in the light of what was to come, it was easier to notice that Rachel, who had begun as a runaway bride with only the dimmest sense of the world beyond Bloomingdale's, was enrolled in a crash course in ordinary life. She was quietly finding her own way in the world, with no husband, no boyfriend, and no heavy-handed parental involvement. *Friends* was a show about six buddies aimlessly sitting around and drinking coffee, but it was also one in which life quietly passed by between refills. Its characters, it hinted, were going to be growing up as they made us laugh.

Rachel and Ross were not the only romance in the show's first season. The very first thing we were shown in Chandler and Joey's apartment was the oversize poster of Laurel and Hardy gracing the back wall. Greg Grande had discovered the poster in the Warner Bros. basement, with little sense that it would become one of the most iconic items of décor on the show. In it, Laurel and Hardy were curled up together in a too-small bed. They were each under the covers, with the diminutive Laurel, his swollen chin held in place by a white cloth that gave the appearance of rabbit ears atop his head, swiveling his eyes to take in his bedmate. The hulking Hardy was leaning on one arm, glowering at his friend with barely disguised hostility over some presumed infraction.

There was a hint of menace in this image—would Hardy really do Laurel some damage with that meaty fist posed in front of the bedcovers?—but it was drowned out by the ludicrousness of their pose. What were they doing in bed together? What had happened to the perpetually unlucky Stan? The poster was an encoded version of the relationship between Chandler and Joey, there to be unlocked by anyone familiar with *Way Out West* or *The Music Box*. Chandler and Joey are not only roommates, but in a kind of platonic gay relationship. David Crane saw Chandler and Joey's friendship as mocking some of the emotional deficiencies of heterosexual male friendship, while also smuggling in gay tropes that might otherwise have found no place in a mainstream sitcom.

Friends was quietly tipping its cap to the mismatched slacker heroes of the early sound era, another celibate same-sex couple prone to all manner of confusions, mishaps, accidents, and small-fry disasters. Chandler and Joey had their other friends, to be sure, but *Friends* was pledging itself—at least at this early stage—to the unity of their partnership. In "The One with the Dozen Lasagnas," Joey and Chandler realize they need a new dining table. Joey and Chandler are a couple in disguise here, their discussion about table shopping an only partially camouflaged conversation about the state of their relationship.

In the next scene, the two men are in a furniture store, where Joey pleads with Chandler to simply pick out a table. Joey rejects a bird pattern after mistakenly selecting a patio-furniture set, and then Chandler turns down some ladybug-themed chairs. "Fine," Joey grouses, "you want to get the birds? Get the birds!" Chandler half turns away, leaning on a wooden chair, and responds like a wife frustrated by her husband's mulishness: "Not like that I won't."

The tenor of the conversation, and the body language, would be instantly familiar to anyone who has ever eavesdropped on a couple fighting in the bedroom section at IKEA. Cut back to their apartment, where the two men, joined by Ross and Monica, crowd around the unseen table. "So, whaddaya think?" asks Chandler. "I think it's the most beautiful table I've ever seen," says Ross as the camera cuts to a shot of their new foosball table. Monica may proceed to wipe the floor with them in their inaugural game, but the foosball table comes to serve as a symbolic stand-in for Chandler and Joey's happily slobbish domestic partnership.

The show spawned its own cult favorites, recurring performers who came in and won the hearts of a dedicated cohort of fans. They were placeholders or temporary solutions to narrative problems that wound up proving more intriguing, or long lasting, than the writers might have initially anticipated, ranging from June Gable as Joey's gravel-voiced agent, Estelle, to Giovanni Ribisi as Phoebe's knucklehead brother, to Paget Brewster as Kathy, a girlfriend of Joey's that Chandler falls for.

During the first season of the show, *Friends'* most popular supporting character was also the one who caused the most dissatisfaction behind the scenes. He was mercurial, prone to unpredictable rages, and untrustworthy as an actor. There was a movement afoot to have him fired from the show, but he was so beloved by audiences that it was hard for *Friends* to let him go. His name was Marcel, and he was a monkey.

Early on, writers Adam Chase and Ira Ungerleider suggested a story line where Ross would adopt a pet to appear more saucy and Mediterranean. Ideas for what kind of animal Ross might take in were batted around, and the writers settled on two options: a monkey and an iguana.

Jeff Strauss had been a biology major in college and had considered becoming a veterinarian. He felt strongly that Ross's getting a monkey would be a major mistake. Strauss launched into a tirade in the writers' room about a monkey making for a ludicrous pet. Monkeys were not cute little people that could be deployed at will to inject some charm into a story line. They spent most of their time masturbating and enjoyed throwing their feces in order to express their dissatisfaction, and what appeared to be a smile was actually a hostile glare.

Strauss lost the battle, and Marcel the monkey was duly introduced as Ross's companion in the tenth episode, "The One with the Monkey." While he didn't love the ways in which Marcel served as Ross's wingman and junior partner, Strauss was relieved that Ross's relationship with the monkey was mostly depicted as an expression of a wounded spirit. Strauss took his children to the zoo and was pleased to hear some of the zookeepers talking to each other about the relative accuracy of the depiction of monkey behavior on the show. It was, Strauss thought, a tiny victory for primate realism.

Almost as soon as Marcel was introduced, the writers of *Friends* were scheming to undo their triumphant mistake. Marcel was wildly popular, and they absolutely hated writing for him. By the time of "The One with Two Parts," Ross was recast as a frustrated father of a reckless son, with Marcel erasing his phone messages and peeing on his newspaper.

Rachel lost Marcel in "The One Where the Monkey Gets Away," and ironically, the monkey got away for real during the episode's preshoot, escaping his handlers and disappearing into the wilds of the stage. With a set that ran four stories high before ascending to the rafters, there was a great deal of ground to cover to coax him back, only further demonstrating the necessity of calling a halt to Marcel's run on the show. Even after he is recovered from the grip of eccentric neighbor Mr. Heckles, who has dressed him in a frilly pink tutu, Ross decides he must send his monkey away to the San Diego Zoo.

Friends rarely went for a self-referential note, but having Marcel come back as a star in the second season's "The One After the Super-bowl," advertising Monkeyshine beer and appearing in a movie with Jean-Claude Van Damme, was a clever gesture in the direction of America's strange love affair with the monkey. *Friends* grew out of its monkey phase, to the point where Ross could offhandedly comment, some seasons later, "Remember when I had a monkey? What was I thinking?"

For "The One with the East German Laundry Detergent," from early in the first season, Phoebe and Chandler were both supposed to break up with the people they were dating. Phoebe would briskly, efficiently, and painlessly end things with her boyfriend, while Chandler, paragon of romantic disaster, would have to endure the worst breakup in human history.

Strauss began to think about what torments Chandler might have to go through and remembered an ex-girlfriend. She had rapidly sought to escalate the relationship far beyond where Strauss was ready to take it. One day, she called up Strauss and told him that she had already purchased his Christmas present. She knew that he collected Fiestaware pottery and had found the ideal piece to add to his collection. She even described to him what it looked like. That it was currently September, or that they had not been out more than two or three times, was no impediment for her. What if Chandler's girlfriend were to bring him a gift just as he was preparing to end things with her? And so Janice (Maggie Wheeler), soon to be Chandler's foil and his relationship Kryptonite, would enter bearing a pair of Bullwinkle socks for him.

Janice was loud and abrasive, her voice less like fingernails on a chalkboard than like a thousand nails scraping on a thousand different chalkboards. Best—or worst—of all was Wheeler's laugh, a braying, wheezing work of art. Janice was not merely a bad date; she was the encapsulation of every bad date anyone had ever had, amplified and exaggerated until the horror became humor. We felt for Chandler that he had been trapped with such an appalling dud, but Janice's presence also telegraphed something essential about Chandler. Chandler was romantically inept, and Janice was here as his comeuppance.

There was no way of knowing it at the time, but Wheeler was to become one of the show's most memorable recurring characters. She turned up again and again when Chandler was weak or bruised, hopeful once more that their wildly mismatched relationship was about to become a romance for the ages. And one of the most charming aspects of Janice's character, and perhaps one that salvaged her from being a stereotype, was just how highly she thought of herself. Janice did not just think she was a catch; she was downright sure of it. And Chandler, for her, was simultaneously the guy who kept breaking her heart and the man who would, one day, make all her dreams come true.

Janice kept showing up long after Chandler had settled down into marriage, there to flirt with Chandler as he attempts to deposit a sperm sample at the doctor's office or planning to buy the home next door when he and Monica move to suburbia. She was, in her own way, a reminder of all the show's many changes, a comedic aide-mémoire regarding the distance from bad romance to real love.

Where Janice was a perpetually braying foghorn, her spiritual counterpart Gunther (James Michael Tyler) was a silent, lurking presence— so much so that he did not have a single line of dialogue until his thirty-third appearance on the show. Tyler was a barista at a Los Angeles coffee shop called the Bourgeois Pig when he was asked to stand in the background and knowledgeably work the levers of the (nonfunctioning) espresso machine at Central Perk. It took two seasons for Tyler to get his first speaking lines, or even a name for his character.

Gunther served as an ongoing running joke for the show, the outsider whose perpetually foiled attempts at penetrating the inner circle emphasized the charmed status of the sextet. Gunther was background color for *Friends*, present at the characters' parties and gatherings, lurking over their shoulders as they sipped coffee at Central Perk. He was there to be ignored and overlooked, forgotten and taken for granted. Gunther was carrying a torch for Rachel while she was only dimly aware of his existence. (At one point, she tells him that one day, he'll make some man very happy.) He was in a perpetual froth of unrequited love and hurt feelings. Gunther was like an upside-down Ross, stymied by his love for a woman, and as a comic doppelgänger, he was obscurely threatened by Ross's very existence. ("What does Rachel see in this guy?" he wonders in voice-over as he serves Ross his coffee.)

Kauffman and Crane had rejected the network's suggestion of a "Pat the Cop," who would dispense mature wisdom to the show's characters, but Gunther was their deliberately askew version of the idea. Gunther offered no insight and no comfort, but he served as a helpful reminder for audiences that, unlike him, we were always welcome to hang out.

CHAPTER 6

THE BIGGEST NEW SHOW ON TV

Creating a Sensation in Season 1

David Crane was out to dinner with his parents and his partner, Jeffrey Klarik, over Thanksgiving weekend in 1994 when Klarik suddenly shushed the conversation. "Listen," he told Crane, directing his attention to a nearby table.

"Did you see the one in the Laundromat?" asked one patron.

"And Ross and Rachel?" responded another.

Klarik told Crane, "Remember this moment. Because the rest will be a blur. But people over there are talking about the show." *Friends* was a show whose fans' enthusiasm could be eavesdropped on.

For many of the people involved with the show, there were discrete moments when their work's impact could be experienced in encounters with strangers. These would be cherished, wrapped in paper to be carried back to the Warner Bros. lot, their good feeling the energy that would drive the grueling work to be done.

Marta Kauffman was out shopping with her child on Larchmont Boulevard, near her home in Hancock Park. A fan spotted her *Friends* hat and approached, asking Kauffman if she might tell her what would happen with Ross and Rachel. She promised she wouldn't tell anyone. On another occasion, Matt LeBlanc was out to lunch with David Schwimmer when a woman spotted Schwimmer. She ran up to their table, practically tossed her baby into Schwimmer's lap, and began frantically digging into her purse in search of a camera so she could take a photograph with him.

Writer and notorious jester Jeff Astrof had a particular coffee shop that he liked getting his coffee from, in no small part because of a pretty waitress named Elizabeth who worked there. Seeking a competitive advantage, Astrof took to chewing meditatively on his pen, staring at his blank notebook page, and musing aloud, "I wonder what Chandler would do?" Elizabeth took the bait and asked Astrof if he was truly a writer for *Friends*. He shyly confirmed that he was, and at the end of a flirtatious conversation, Astrof told her, "I think Chandler will date a girl named Elizabeth."

Astrof brought the story back to the room, as much to share a funny story as to brag, and Crane topped the joke with an acidulous put-down, delivered with as much stern force as he could muster: "Chandler would never date *anyone* named Elizabeth." (Of course, years later, *Ross* would date someone named Elizabeth, but by then Astrof and his waitress crush were long gone.)

In March, near the end of the first season, the cast of *Friends* was summoned for the closest thing to an American version of a royal audience. The six actors were to appear on *The Oprah Winfrey Show* and bathe in the glow of Oprah's love. The appearance would require them to fly to Chicago, and Courteney Cox initially balked, suggesting she would appear via satellite. David Schwimmer, the defender of cast unity above all, insisted that they all appear in person, and Cox agreed to come.

Before the shoot, some of the actors quickly huddled together to discuss how they might respond to the concerns about *Friends*' overwhelming whiteness, which had been a regular subject of media coverage. What would they tell Oprah about why there were no black friends, and moreover, about the lack of diversity on the show in general?

As it turned out, Oprah referenced the racial concerns with delicacy, transforming it into a joke. "I'd like y'all to get a black friend," Winfrey told them. "Maybe I could stop by. In fact, I'm thinking about buying that apartment building next door." Winfrey told the cast that fans were gathering together in groups to watch the show, and Kudrow, for one, was flabbergasted. Apparently the show was a hit. She knew the ratings were good, but ensconced in their bubble on the Warner Bros. lot, she did not realize how passionately Americans were responding to *Friends*.

Crane was taken aback to spot the cast of the show on the cover of *Rolling Stone* in May 1995. He began calculating how much time had passed between shooting the show's pilot and his cast's appearance on the cover of one of the most prominent magazines in the United States. How long ago had it been that Crane had been kept up nights over his worries regarding whether the show would be canceled or not picked up, or whether he would be fired?

It had felt downright greedy to hope for a second season of the show, and now here they were, in the white-hot center of American popular culture, riding in a vintage automobile while kitted out in 1940s retro chic—Schwimmer in a sailor's uniform, Cox in a plunging strapless floral-print, and Perry, eyes bulging, casting an alarmed glance at her while wearing a jaunty straw hat.

Ratings had steadily crept up over the course of the season, from a low 20s share (the percentage of viewers watching television at that hour who were watching *Friends*) for the first handful of episodes to a share consistently at or above 30 for the final third of the season, which ranked it among the most successful series on TV. And summer, when NBC broadcast reruns of the show, allowed fans who had missed out on the beginning of *Friends* to catch up, with ratings ascending even higher.

Adam Chase went home to New Jersey to visit his parents in the interval between seasons, and on his return to Los Angeles, he passed by an airport newsstand filled with *Friends*-themed covers. His first thought was that editors at these magazines were likely going to be in trouble for running such similar covers simultaneously. His second thought was that his show must suddenly have become a huge hit.

The media's enthusiasm was indicative of a shift in cultural attitudes toward television stars. Prior to *Friends*, there had been a certain ingrained belief in the second-tier status of television stardom. The gathering frenzy around the six stars of *Friends* began the process of resetting what TV stardom might look like. Schwimmer, Aniston, Cox, Perry, LeBlanc, and Kudrow might only have been television stars, but the depth and passion of fans' interest in their new favorites exceeded that directed at any other stars of the mid-1990s.

Old habits were hard to kill off, and an inordinate amount of the media's coverage of *Friends* revolved around a single question: Which of the show's stars were likely to become movie stars? The actors were treated like minor-league baseball phenoms who had won themselves an invitation to the Big Show. The coverage inevitably diminished the scope of *Friends*' accomplishment, treating it like an interim success whose significance would be wiped out if none of its stars could make the leap to movie acting. But all six actors were indeed intent on using *Friends* as a springboard to movie stardom. The summer of 1995, when the show was on hiatus, rapidly filled up with scheduled movie shoots intended to launch the show's performers into the stratosphere.

Schwimmer starred in the *Graduate*-esque romantic comedy *The Pallbearer*, LeBlanc appeared opposite a chimpanzee in the baseball film *Ed*, and Aniston won a plum role in *She's the One*, director Edward Burns's follow-up to the acclaimed *The Brothers McMullen*. None were hits, nor was Matthew Perry's attempt to vault to leading-man status with the romantic comedy *Fools Rush In*, opposite Salma Hayek, one year later.

The only *Friends* star to meet with immediate cinematic success was the one who had already experienced it. Courteney Cox turned in a solid performance as a reporter in Wes Craven's self-referential horror film *Scream*, which wound up grossing over $100 million at the domestic box office in 1996. Journalists pored over the results with the nuance of elderly Talmudists, intent on parsing the meaning of the message being sent by the American moviegoing populace. Did fans not want to pay to see the *Friends* stars play roles too similar to the ones available for free on network television? Did they not want to see them at all after twenty-four episodes?

The obsessive coverage of the movie transition mostly overlooked two primary facts. First, the *Friends* stars' movies had mostly flopped because they had been inept. They had not been sunk by the lesser wattage of a television actor's stardom. The one that had succeeded, *Scream*, had featured a clever concept, an appealing cast, and a talented director, and had not been sold as "*Friends*, but at the multiplex." And Cox had been a supporting performer, not a stand-alone star. Second, the stars of *Friends*, even after their movie careers' collective failures to launch, were still enormous stars. It was only the stubborn insistence that movie stardom was genuine currency and television stardom counterfeit that made this a subject for consideration.

Warner Bros. and NBC scheduled an avalanche of tie-ins and promotions to cash in on the *Friends* frenzy. There were plans for everything from *Friends*-themed calendars to a *Friends* coffee line. Turn on the TV, and there they were—in character—hawking Diet Coke. Turn on the radio, and that familiar theme song was now omnipresent, dominating the charts.

Coca-Cola approached the showrunners with an amount of money that was hard to turn away from. Crane and Kauffman put the writers to work for an entire week drafting ideas for the Diet Coke commercials, in which the six friends would tout the wonders of the low-calorie soda. The showrunners were still in the first blush of success and inclined to snatch at every business opportunity that came their way, but as Crane and Kauffman both later acknowledged, the commercials were a notable misstep. Kevin Bright, too, believed that the unneeded complexity of the commercials—why did the performers have to appear as their *Friends* characters, rather than as themselves?—fed into the burgeoning *Friends* backlash.

In one commercial, the six friends appeared in a police lineup, swearing their innocence regarding the theft of a missing Diet Coke. In another thirty-second spot, each was interrogated, with Phoebe suggesting candles to lighten the hard-boiled atmosphere and Monica ranting about how she had no alibi because she did not have a boyfriend.

The commercials were perfectly adequate, in and of themselves, but their crass hucksterism felt at odds with *Friends'* warmth. Crane later argued that not only had he put the show at risk by taking the Diet Coke commercials, he had put the actors in a difficult spot by encouraging them to take the gig. Of all the choices he had made over the course of a decade running *Friends*, it was the one he wanted back most.

Kevin Bright had become impressed with the work of the Hasidic Jewish sect Chabad and offered to freshen up their annual telethon to raise money for their drug-and-alcohol-rehabilitation centers, which usually leaned to guest appearances by the likes of Shelley Berman, by cajoling the cast to appear. (The video is worth tracking down, if only to listen to Matt LeBlanc attempt to pronounce *Chabad*.) Matthew Perry and Jennifer Aniston shot a commercial for Windows 95, in which a prototypical tech geek told them "communicating online is the hot thing right now." And Kudrow, Cox, and Aniston filmed a promotional video for the NBA from Monica and Rachel's living room, in which they betrayed a vaguely erotic enthusiasm for old-school NBA short-shorts and swooned over—of all unlikely people—Utah Jazz point guard John Stockton. *Friends'* sudden ubiquity meant that its characters were inescapable, which was not necessarily desirable for a hit show intent on staying popular for years to come.

———

Oprah Winfrey may have delicately tiptoed around it, but the question of *Friends'* lack of diversity remained a recurrent critique of the show. How could a show set in Manhattan be so lily-white? A drumbeat of articles in the mainstream media after the show's first season castigated *Friends* not only for featuring six white protagonists, but for depicting "a fictional Manhattan where black people are strangely absent from restaurants, museums, health clubs and the streets."

While network dramas like *ER* and *Homicide: Life on the Street* included integrated casts and racially incisive plotlines, comedies like *Friends* rarely featured nonwhite characters, even in supporting or one-off roles. Jonathan Storm of *The Philadelphia Inquirer* totted up the numbers in a 1996 article, determining that of the sixty-four comedies that had appeared on any of the six networks during that season, only twelve had featured racially mixed casts, with forty all-white and twelve all-black shows comprising the remainder.

Friends, third in the Nielsen ratings, ranked ninety-ninth in African-American households. It was telling that *Friends* was programmed in the same time slot as *Living Single*, the Fox sitcom about single African-American women frequently mentioned as a precursor to *Friends*. The *Inquirer* spoke to Brown University professor Sasha Torres, who described *Friends* and its network counterparts as "figuratively and narratively trying to make urban spaces safe for white people." This phenomenon was not exclusive to *Friends* but was predicated on the domestic intimacy of comedy.

"The comedies for some reason just have not been courageous," *ER* executive producer John Wells told the *Los Angeles Times*. "I certainly was determined to do our show with a multiracial and multicultural focus. It's irresponsible not to. It does not mirror the society we live in."

Friends would later address its racial deficiencies by casting Gabrielle Union in a one-off role as a woman Ross and Joey simultaneously date in the seventh season, and Aisha Tyler as a paleontologist attracted to Joey in the ninth and tenth seasons. (There had also been the Asian-American Lauren Tom as Ross's love interest Julie in the second season.) Much of the media's attention, when it came to matters of diversity in the 1990s and early 2000s, was concentrated on the proportion of African-American actors cast in key roles, and the criticism of *Friends* often took the shape of wondering when the show would feature an African-American performer in a major role. The effort was notable, if demonstrably tardy, but USC professor Todd Boyd described it in a 2003 *Boston Globe* article as "a slap in the face. . . . They're saying, 'We'll do this when we know we're going off the air. We've addressed the critics, now leave us alone.'" *Friends* never really had much of an answer for its whiteness, and its reflexive defensiveness when the subject was broached only increased the sense of discomfort. The show had countless opportunities to improve its track record on diverse casting and mostly failed to respond to the very legitimate critique being proffered.

Friends could not be solely blamed for what had been a preexisting condition on television. But *Friends'* enormous success prompted a rash of imitators intent on similar all-white ensembles, according to Mike Duffy of the *Chicago Tribune*: "The trend has become only more pronounced this season, with the 'Friends' phenomenon sparking a whitebread wave of sitcom clones about young Caucasian chuckleheads."

NBC offered two more urban-living comedies, *Caroline in the City* and *The Single Guy*, in 1995, and ABC and Fox had their own attempts at replicating Central Perk. *The Washington Post's* Tom Shales saw *Friends* as the harbinger of a newly crude era on television and was disturbed by its replicating itself across the network lineup. Shales was resigned to endless *Friends* imitators, but no one was going to get him to chuckle over it: "This year's new hit is certain to inspire the networks to send in the clones. It's the eternal cycle of TV Land—or rather the eternal recycle."

Perhaps the most powerful indicator of *Friends'* remarkable success was what it inspired Charlie Quinn to do. Quinn, the program director at a Nashville radio station, pulled the forty-five-second version of the *Friends* theme song off the telecast and looped it until he had a three-minute song he could play on the air. "I'll Be There for You" rapidly became a runaway hit, and the impromptu song spread from Tennessee around the country.

Friends had made the Rembrandts suddenly famous, but at first, the duo was uninterested in recording a full-length version of the theme song. The money in music was in songwriting, and the band did not want to record someone else's work. The band's record label, East West Records, insisted, threatening that without "I'll Be There for You," they wouldn't release the band's new album. A compromise was ultimately worked out, and the Rembrandts—Danny Wilde and Phil Solem—were cut in as cowriters of the fuller song, which added new lyrics to the original version, along with Kauffman, Crane, Skloff, and veteran songwriter Allee Willis.

The full-length version of "I'll Be There for You" became a breakout hit in 1995, cracking the top twenty on the *Billboard* charts. The song became the centerpiece of the Rembrandts' album *L.P.*, as well as a *Friends* tie-in soundtrack album, which spliced juicy bits of the show's dialogue with songs by Hootie & the Blowfish, R.E.M., and Paul Westerberg.

———

David Crane had felt little additional pressure heading into the second season. There was a show to be written, and no one's opinion mattered to him other than those of the people in the room and the people on the set. Whether *Friends* was an enormous hit or an underachiever, the problems remained the same: What was our story? How would we get the audience to care? *Friends* might have been one of the top-rated shows on television, it might have occupied far more than its fair share of space on newsstands across America, but work was work, and there would be little to no discussion of *Friends* the phenomenon on the set or in the writers' room. Others noticed changes, though. The stars now had security guards. There were luxury cars in the employee parking lot and discussions of the new homes the cast and crew were buying.

For Crane, *Friends* was merely a television program that employed a group of serious, efficient, and talented people, one of whose many responsibilities was to entirely tune out any and all discussion of the show that took place outside of work. It was remarkable to Crane simply that the show continued to air and that NBC was placing its confidence in their work.

Crane and Kauffman may have been of one mind in their insistence on keeping success at bay, but the executives charged with fostering the show's development did not always heed their message. After the second-season premiere, in which Ross introduced his new girlfriend Julie (Lauren Tom) to the group, Les Moonves, then president of Warner Bros. Television (and soon to become head of a rival network, CBS), came to the *Friends* soundstage and read the show's Nielsen ratings to the cast and crew. Moonves was celebrating *Friends*' remarkable numbers, the strongest indication yet that NBC had another huge hit on its hands. Adam Chase turned to a colleague and said, "I don't know what those numbers mean, but I've never seen this guy before. I think this is a big deal."

Everyone wanted to benefit from the extraordinary popularity of the show, not least among them James Burrows. Burrows had directed the pilot, his imprimatur an enormous help in convincing others to take its chances more seriously. He had found his way to the emotional and comedic heart of the show, and had swiftly and wisely directed it toward the Ross-and-Rachel plot arc that would serve the show for a decade to come. Burrows was already a sitcom veteran where most everyone else associated with the show was a relative newcomer, and when *Friends* became an enormous hit, he expected to be cut in for his fair share of the show's profits.

There were two complaints about Burrows, one large and one relatively small, that prevented this from happening and resulted in his mostly ceasing to direct new episodes of *Friends* after the first season. The small complaint was significant enough. It came courtesy of Kevin Bright and others on the *Friends* team who felt that while Burrows was undeniably a sitcom wizard and had a remarkable gift for understanding comedy, he was always in a hurry. The first take was always perfect in his eyes, and the entire episode, complete with pauses for the writers to adjust lines, would be wrapped by ten P.M. each week—still late by sitcom standards, but downright early in comparison to what would come on *Friends*. Burrows enjoyed maintaining a limber, quick-paced set where the show's creators would often have preferred to slow down and take notice of how best to improve the final product, even if it took substantially longer.

The proof was in the pudding, and the final results were undeniably good, but Burrows seemed to be in a hurry to get to his vacation home in Mexico each Tuesday night, and this caused resentment among some of the people putting in punishing hours to make *Friends*. It was not that the show suffered under Burrows's watch; it palpably did not. But there was a growing sense that there were opportunities Burrows was leaving behind in his haste to finish each week.

Kevin Bright was the one in the editing bay putting each episode together, and he saw where directors could improve the final product by shooting more or by using different camera setups. Burrows was a superlative director, everyone agreed. But Bright was not only a director; he was also a producer, an editor, and a showrunner, and he wanted to take greater ownership over the shoot itself. It was telling that Bright himself directed the first-season finale, "The One Where Rachel Finds Out." Bright would direct many more episodes in the future.

The larger concern was, as large concerns often are, about money. There was only so much money to go around, and for Burrows to get a big enough piece of the *Friends* pie, Crane, Kauffman, and Bright would have to give up some of what they were to earn. They all liked James Burrows and were appreciative of all he had done to make *Friends* a success. They also agreed that this was their baby and Burrows, while extremely helpful, had played only a small part in its creation. As long as Burrows was around, *Friends* ran the risk of being treated as another show in the distinguished lineage of Jimmy Burrows smash hits. Kevin Bright in particular felt confident that the show would thrive in Burrows's absence just as it had in his presence and was anxious for them to stake a claim for *Friends* as theirs.

Nobody wanted Burrows to leave *Friends* permanently, including Burrows himself, and so room was made for him to come back occasionally after the first season. He would direct the classic "The One with the

Prom Video" in the second season, and three more episodes in the years that followed. When Burrows returned, he would insist on bringing back the wooden post and beam that had served as a separation pillar between the kitchen and living room in Monica and Rachel's apartment, which had been subtly jettisoned after the first season. Burrows preferred having it as visual decoration for his shots, and so the crew would have to lug it out from whatever forgotten storage closet it had been abandoned in since the last time Burrows had been on set.

NBC was insistent on featuring its hottest series in its most important showcase: the slot immediately following the Super Bowl. NBC was going to be broadcasting the game in 1996 and wanted to display its most impressive wares for the captive audience already tuning in to the game. Crane and Kauffman received a call from NBC informing them that they were to receive the plum post–Super Bowl slot. Crane and Kauffman thought it over and determined that given both the length and the time slot, it would not be enough to simply broadcast a traditional episode of the show. They would have to deliver something bigger.

The show recruited a host of famous guest stars, including Brooke Shields, Jean-Claude Van Damme, Chris Isaak, and Julia Roberts, to appear on the hour-long "The One After the Superbowl." Shields would be a delusional stalker who believes that Joey really is his *Days of Our Lives* character, Dr. Drake Ramoray. Van Damme would play himself, with Rachel and Monica squabbling over him after they encounter him on a movie set. Isaak would be a librarian love interest for Phoebe. And Roberts would play an old friend of Chandler's who gets payback for a childhood prank.

Producer Todd Stevens had managed to assemble a mock action-film set on the outdoor back lot, complete with burning cars and vehicles flipped on their sides. The whole effort felt very much like a Van Damme production—unusual for a show generally not particularly committed to veracity or realism.

Director Michael Lembeck was taken aback to spot Brooke Shields's then-boyfriend Andre Agassi arriving on the set with a hulking bodyguard. Agassi and his bodyguard were sitting disconcertingly close to the set as Shields ran through the scene in which she licked Matt Le-Blanc's hand. As soon as Lembeck called cut, Agassi rushed the set and tore into Shields, humiliating her and reducing her to tears before storming out. It was left to Lembeck, along with the cast, to lift Shields's spirits and encourage her to carry on.

Even Julia Roberts—at that point close to the biggest star in the world—lost some of her self-confidence when it came time to face the audience on the Friday evening they were to shoot the episode. Roberts had not been in front of a live audience since she was a teenager, and she was now squeezing Lembeck's hand fiercely. While the director could feel his bones being crushed, he understood his responsibility in the moment was to guide her through it as best he could.

She went out for her first scene with Perry, and while Lembeck massaged his gangrenous hand, he watched her perform. Lembeck felt that if a word bubble could have been appended to her first take, it would have read, "Wait a minute, I can do this!" The second take was superb, but it required her getting through that first take and regaining the confidence needed to face an audience. Stealing Chandler's clothes and then taunting him in a restaurant bathroom, Roberts contributed some of the funniest moments of a deeply uneven episode.

Van Damme showed up for the shoot twelve hours late. What had been scheduled to be a morning shoot with Van Damme on the mock film set was now taking place in the evening, with a very un-*Friends*-like nighttime look to accommodate the new circumstances. Lembeck had his hands full simply coaching Van Damme through his few lines of dialogue and keeping him from disturbing his female costars.

"The One After the Superbowl" wound up as the most-watched episode in the show's history, with 52.9 million viewers, but was hardly the ideal introduction to the show. It was a reminder that the second season of *Friends* was not the first, and could never be. The first season had been an unexpected triumph; the second time around, critics were gunning for the show, and *Friends* was opening the door to criticism with lesser efforts like "Superbowl." With bloated enterprises like this episode, *Friends* was playing into the hands of critics carping about the show's lowest-common-denominator impulses. Some of this was the blowback that any popular TV show would engender, but some was also prompted by *Friends'* desire to please everyone all the time.

In retrospect, Crane thought the Super Bowl episode was a tremendous opportunity, but one whose final shape did not entirely resemble the show. *Friends* occupied its own rarefied space in American popular culture, one that not only did not need any infusions of star power but could be hindered by stars not up to the caliber, or popularity, of its own performers.

Part of *Friends'* lesser critical status stemmed from its reputation as a photocopy of *Seinfeld*, a pale WASP knockoff. While *Friends* was less groundbreaking a comedy than *Seinfeld*, the particulars of its reputation were misguided. *Seinfeld* was known as an echt-Jewish show, with its fixation on babkas and Upper West Side schlemiels, but the series masked its obviously Jewish characters as other ethnic types. (George is Italian? Costanza, please.)

Friends, by contrast, was more forthright about the ethnic backgrounds of its characters, with Rachel, Ross, and Monica all pegged as Jews of varying types. (Ross and Monica were supposed to be half-Jewish.) Their Jewishness came out most strongly in the flashback episodes, with Ross in his Jewfro and Rachel with her pre-rhinoplasty nose; to be Jewish was, in *Friends'* eyes, to be geeky and unpolished.

The show was required to regularly contort itself in response to the question of what it could and could not say on network television. One of David Crane's most important weekly tasks was his conversation with NBC's standards division. He customarily took the calls in the writers' room, happy to let his staff hear just some of what was required to get their vision to air.

Crane would negotiate over whether he was allotted one *breast* or two in a given episode's dialogue. *Asshole* was verboten, but *ass* was allowed. For a time, NBC banned *Friends* from using the word *penis*, before changing their minds and allowing it again. At other times, the concern was about tonnage. Two mentions of *penis* would be OK, but three was unacceptable. Kauffman and Crane had gotten their television education with HBO, and this sudden outburst of middle-school morality was frustrating.

Could Monica and Rachel be shown squabbling over the last condom in the bathroom drawer? Could a condom wrapper be shown on a bedside table? Kauffman and Crane were perpetually frustrated with the degree of pushback *Friends* received from NBC, especially when compared with *Seinfeld*, which could devote an entire episode to a masturbation contest. Initially, Kauffman and Crane were told that the distinction between the two shows stemmed from when they aired. *Friends*, airing before nine o'clock, attracted a younger audience that NBC had to be mindful of.

Even when *Friends* shifted to nine thirty late in the first season, NBC's attitude hardly budged. When Crane pushed back, NBC executives told him that, having attracted a younger audience, the network was fearful of alienating youthful *Friends* fans by having its characters say and do things that would provoke discomfort.

In response, *Friends* perfected a side glance at raunchy material, avoiding the kind of explicit dialogue that might run into difficulties with Standards and Practices. *Friends* managed the feat of making sex feel wholesome and all-American, a necessary stage in the evolution of the American adult. Sex was the ocean in which *Friends*' characters swam, with actual depictions of sex eschewed in favor of torrents of sexual talk. Conversation was the thing *Friends* enjoyed most, and what could be better to talk about than sex?

Intriguingly, sex talk was never treated as exclusively the province of the men on the show. *Friends*' female characters were allowed to be casually sexual. Don Ohlmeyer had worried that audiences would judge Monica for her perceived sluttishness, but he had read the crowd wrong. *Friends'* fans were comfortable with equal-opportunity sexual banter.

In a memorable sequence in "The One with Phoebe's Uterus," Monica walks the clueless Chandler through women's seven erogenous zones, laying out one potential sequence by chanting numbers with increasing fervor. "Seven! Seven! Seven!" she shouts before lying back, spent by the encounter with her imagination. After Monica accidentally knocks her nephew Ben's head against a post and encourages Rachel to similarly clobber her head in an effort to soothe him, Rachel coyly notes, "If it's not a headboard, it's just not worth it."

As with Chandler and Joey, much of the sexual banter was actually character banter in disguise, merely another facet of their intimate (at times almost intrusive) knowledge of each other's preferences, peccadilloes, and pet peeves. There would later be easy jokes to be mined about naked prostitutes at Chandler's bachelor party, but there was also a character joke about Joey's presuming that the horror of spending day after day with the same woman would soon have him longing for "the sweet release of death." And it would be sexual banter transformed into character study that would grant *Friends* one of its most enduring episodes, and a notable moment in the depiction of sexuality on American television.

———

In the fall of 1995, Candace Gingrich was traveling the country as part of the Coming Out Project, which educated young people about gay rights, reminded them of the progress yet to be made, and offered those still in the closet a safe space in which to acknowledge their sexuality.

She was just back from one Coming Out Project trip when a colleague came up to her with a message: "You got a phone call from *Friends*. They want you to be on the show." "Shut the fuck up," Gingrich replied. "That's not funny. Don't mess with me like that." Once Gingrich was finally convinced *Friends* had actually called, she got in touch with a producer on the show, who explained that they were shooting a lesbian wedding and wanted to cast Gingrich as the officiant. Could she fly out to Los Angeles tomorrow?

Friends was returning to Ross's ex-wife Carol and her partner Susan (Jessica Hecht) with a charming episode devoted to their wedding. For those aware of who she was, the presence of Candace Gingrich on *Friends* was a reminder that there were people in the real world who were only too happy to paint this loving union between two women as the source of all societal dysfunction. Candace was Speaker of the House Newt Gingrich's half sister and had been taken aback, but not surprised, by some comments her brother had recently made about homosexuality, in which he had argued that "it is madness to pretend that families are anything other than heterosexual couples."

David Crane was pleased to have someone known in her own right for her advocacy on behalf of gay rights but also enjoyed the gentle political commentary of employing the sister of the homophobic Speaker of the House to officiate at the most famous (imaginary) lesbian wedding in the history of the United States. Only the preceding month, *Roseanne* had featured a wedding between two of its gay characters, giving the two shows an opportunity to introduce American television to a kind of love that had never before graced prime time. It was telling that in both instances, the gay characters would be in supporting roles; it would not be until 1997 that Ellen DeGeneres would come out on *Ellen*.

There would be no full week of rehearsal for Gingrich, as many of the professional performers asked to appear on the show had gotten. She showed up on the day of the shoot and almost immediately filmed her scenes. During the filming of the reception sequence, Gingrich was standing near Matt LeBlanc, who leaned over and thanked her for appearing and for speaking out about gay and lesbian issues. He had been raised by a single mother, he told her, who had instilled in him a belief in respecting differences.

"The One with the Lesbian Wedding" devotes the bulk of its running time to other plotlines, but the segment devoted to the nuptials is bittersweet and delicate. Carol suffers from a last-minute case of cold feet and thinks of calling off the wedding. It is left to Ross to talk her out of it: "This is your wedding. Do it." The implication, an especially generous one coming from her ex-husband, is that this wedding will be hers in a way that their wedding could never have been. Ross winds up walking Carol down the aisle, in one of the most emotionally nourishing beats of the Ross-Carol plotline. Before *Ellen*'s coming-out episode, before *Will & Grace*, during the first term of a president soon to sign the punitive Defense of Marriage Act, *Friends* was staking its claim to the telling of emotionally complex queer stories.

Friends is not above jokes about the idea of a lesbian wedding, but these are grounded in parodying heterosexual self-absorption. Joey takes in the scene at the wedding and despairs: "It just seems so futile. All these women and—nothing. I feel like Superman without my powers." Chandler responds with one of the best lines of the series, and a perfect summation of his mind-set: "The world is my lesbian wedding." The episode even finds room for a sweet moment between David Schwimmer and Jessica Hecht, with Susan approaching Ross to offer a rare bit of praise: "You did a good thing today. You wanna dance?" Susan offers to let him lead, and they take to the floor to the strains of "Strangers in the Night." Hecht, who sometimes struggled to understand *Friends*' sense of humor regarding her character, loved the scene, finding it a charming respite from the perpetual air of hostility between Susan and Ross.

In retrospect, Crane wished that he had dared to tell "The One with the Lesbian Wedding" from the perspective of the women getting married and not from that of the possessive, jealous ex-husband. A more contemporary sensibility would have demanded it, but the resulting episode was tender and genuine nonetheless.

And *Friends* would later sneakily pay homage to same-sex love, with a single throwaway moment from the end of the third season's "The One

Without the Ski Trip" speaking to *Friends'* quiet frankness. Ross knocked on his ex Carol's door late at night, and Carol answered, flustered and in the midst of cinching her robe shut. She was not sleeping, she tells Ross, and as she does so, her tongue flicks past her teeth, and she reaches up to remove a pubic hair from her mouth. The gesture was unscripted and served as a reminder of Carol and Susan as sexual beings in their own right.

NBC prepared for a deluge of viewer complaints about "Lesbian Wedding" that never arrived. The network hired 104 operators to field calls, and wound up receiving a grand total of 2 complaints that evening. A month later, Reverend Donald Wildmon's acolytes sent in letters of complaint, but the letters made it clear they had not watched the episode in question. NBC affiliates in Ohio and Texas, among others, chose not to air the episode out of fear of the tender sensibilities of their viewers, but those who did watch "The One with the Lesbian Wedding" seemed mostly unfazed by the experience.

It was not until after the episode was aired, and Jane Sibbett was appearing with the likes of Geraldo Rivera to discuss it, that she realized how significant it might be for lesbians who had never seen themselves represented on television before. How much more would it have done for them, Sibbett wondered, if Carol and Susan had also been able to kiss like any other newlyweds?

Sibbett had been raised in a religious home and attended a Presbyterian church in Hollywood at the time she won the role of Carol. Her father had grown more conservative as he aged, and he began hosting a weekly Bible-study class in his home on Thursday nights to ensure that none of his friends would see his daughter playing a lesbian on TV. After "The One with the Lesbian Wedding" aired, she began hearing from many fellow congregants from her childhood, who were writing to tell her she was going to hell. Sibbett was confounded by the response and sad for the childhood friends who had worked themselves up into such a frenzy over the idea of others' happiness.

Some time later, Sibbett would be called, along with Hecht, to accept an award on behalf of *Friends* from an organization that supported gay families. The group's president rose to speak and observed that if he had been able to see characters like Carol and Susan on television when he had been a child, he might not have attempted suicide on multiple occasions. "The One with the Lesbian Wedding" was imperfect, but its imperfections were embraced by countless people hungering for something that reminded them of themselves on American television.

Friends was more than another television show now. In its embrace of the aggressively normal in its storytelling, it was able to expand the spectrum of normalcy until it could also include a lesbian wedding. Television had the power to change minds.

CHAPTER 7

LOBSTERS

The Ballad of Ross and Rachel, Part 1

The ebbs and flows of Ross and Rachel's relationship would become numerous, and famous, enough to form their own shorthand language: The kiss in the rain. "We were on a break." The eighteen-page letter. "I, Ross, take thee, Rachel." The Las Vegas wedding and the delayed divorce.

There would be ten seasons of diversions, interludes, setbacks, and warfare in total, interspersed with occasional outbursts of romance, before the inevitable, but much-needed, satisfying conclusion. *Cheers'* Sam and Diane, sparring and smooching for five seasons, had set the previous record for maximal sitcom delayed gratification, but Ross and Rachel's delayed happy ending set what is likely an unbreakable record for holding off on the inevitable.

And so *Friends* became something it never expected to be: a master class in postponement. At every turn, when it seemed like each possible impediment to Ross and Rachel's reunion had been removed, another roadblock magically appeared. *Friends* was intended to offer viewers an uncomplicated pleasure. And yet, so much of that pleasure was about withholding the very thing fans wanted most. The ballad of Ross and Rachel was rarely sad, although there were moments where, like some of the show's characters, we were expected to weep over their missed opportunities. But their romance was intended to serve as the tart, occasionally bitter counterpoint to the show's sweet comedy.

The conclusion of *Friends'* first season had moved Rachel and Ross closer than they had ever been to love, and also further away. Just as Rachel learned of Ross's feelings for her, Ross was off in China, meeting and falling for his colleague Julie. In an abrupt switch, *Friends* inverted its central romantic partnership, with Rachel silently pining and Ross obliviously swanning.

Only Ross would think it was a good idea to go on to his ex-crush, in the second-season opener, "The One with Ross's New Girlfriend," about how she was so "funny and sweet and amazing and adorable." Rachel is now the neurotic and antic one, grabbing the phone out of Ross's hands as he babbles sweet nothings to Julie and abruptly hanging it up, or attempting to convince him that the sexiest thing he could do would be to delay having sex with his girlfriend.

Rachel's jealousy is an unexpected new aspect of her personality and allows the seemingly endless pas de deux of buried emotions to reach a graceful conclusion early in the second season, in "The One Where Ross Finds Out." Rachel goes out on a date and drunkenly borrows another diner's cell phone to call Ross. She leaves a sloppy, strangely triumphant message for him: "Obviously I am over you. I am over you, and that, my friend, is what they call 'closure.'" Spent and sated, she proceeds to toss the cell phone into a nearby ice bucket.

The next morning, a hungover Rachel is hazy on the details of the previous evening, but when Ross begins listening to his voice mail, she belatedly realizes the enormity of her drunken gaffe and leaps onto Ross's back in the hope of wrestling the phone away from his ear. She succeeds in knocking the phone out of his grasp, but it is too late: "You're over me? You're over me? When—when were you . . . under me?"

Aniston has a lovely moment here, moaning and covering her face while summoning the courage to acknowledge her emotional turmoil. She looks down and fusses with a couch pillow while haltingly telling Ross, "Lately, I've, uh, I've sort of had feelings for you." Rachel is breathing hard, nervously blowing her hair out of her face. When Ross asks her, "Now you're over me?" she responds with a soft, breathy question of her own: "Are you over me?" The moment is interrupted by Julie, who is ringing the buzzer and waiting with a taxi down below.

Ross bursts into Central Perk after hours in the next scene, overwrought from the emotional turmoil, and blames Rachel for revealing her feelings just as he was settling in with Julie. "This ship has sailed," he tells Rachel, and runs off, leaving Rachel crying on the couch.

Aniston is the most appealingly vulnerable of the *Friends* performers, and we feel her hurt in this scene, rejected and trampled and embarrassed all at once. Her sobbing catches Ross's eye as well, as he looks in from outside Central Perk's window. The two stare at each other for a long moment, and Rachel tentatively approaches the door. She briefly battles with a tempestuous lock before swinging both doors wide open. Ross and Rachel kiss in the misty Manhattan rain, Rachel's hands tenderly caressing his face.

Friends always had an innate sense of its audience's desires and a compulsion to fulfill its unspoken promises. The audience had been promised a resolution, and "The One Where Ross Finds Out" delivers. But the show was torn between what its audience wanted and what it was best at, and nowhere was this disjunction clearer than in its handling of Ross and Rachel's romance. The audience, presumably, would have been more than satisfied for the couple to live happily ever after, but almost as soon as *Friends* provided a successful conclusion, it began to walk it back.

Ross, still intellectually torn between Rachel and Julie, begins crafting a pros-and-cons list, observing that Rachel is ditzy, obsessed with her looks, and just a waitress. He is inevitably caught by Rachel, who is appalled at seeing her deficiencies spelled out so openly: "Imagine the worst things you think about yourself. Now how would you feel if the one person that you trusted the most in the world not only thinks them too, but actually uses them as reasons *not* to be with you?" Ross, an oblivious doofus to the last, charmlessly pleads his case: "I want to be with you in spite of all those things." Rachel is disgusted, and the possibility of their romance appears to fizzle. (Much like the close of the first season, in which Jeff Greenstein had borrowed from Jane Austen to bring Ross and Rachel closer together, this plot development bears notable similarities to Mr. Darcy's first proposal in *Pride and Prejudice*.)

It would take the revelations of "The One with the Prom Video," midway through the second season, to silently plead Ross's case for him, and for Rachel to fully overcome her reservations about Ross. At the start of the episode, Ross listens patiently to Phoebe's explanation of how elderly lobsters hold each other's claws in the tank. She argues that he and Rachel are each other's lobsters. When Ross fumblingly attempts to explain Phoebe's theory to Rachel, she walks off: "We are never going to happen. Accept that."

Later in the episode, when Monica is sorting through childhood bric-a-brac excavated from her parents' house, she comes across a videotape from high school, which she slips into her VCR. Rachel is in a ruffled blue prom dress, her nose markedly larger than it appears now. "How do you zoom out?" we hear Monica's father call out as the camera settles on his daughter's zaftig frame. Cox had to be molded into a specially designed fat suit for the sequence, a process that took hours and left her a sweaty mess by the end of the shoot.

"Some girl ate Monica!" Joey blurts.

"Shut up!" Monica shouts. "The camera adds ten pounds."

Chandler famously responds by asking, "So how many cameras are actually on you?"

Director James Burrows brought in camcorders to shoot the home-video sequence, dirtying the image with extra noise to give it the feel of an old home movie. Producer Todd Stevens was pleased with Aniston's fake nose but felt that Schwimmer's wig and mustache had the perverse effect of making him look older, not younger.

What initially appears to be a ludicrous flashback is actually a cleverly disguised emotional moment. Ross instantly recognizes the videotape, his face clearly registering that reliving this particular memory will likely be agonizing.

The comedy is not quite over yet, as adolescent Ross makes his first appearance on the screen, with a scraggly mustache and a lush Jewfro. ("Looking good, Mr. Kotter!" Joey calls out, in a joke that likely registers with precisely none of *Friends*' millennial audience.)

When Rachel's date fails to show, Ross's mother suggests that the then-college-aged Ross take her to the prom. We see Ross tripping on his way up the stairs, but there is an emotional charge to spotting him in his father's tuxedo, giving himself a pep talk to "just be cool" as he holds a bouquet of flowers grabbed from a vase.

Ross comes down the stairs just as Rachel and Monica and their dates, their backs to him, troop out the door. Rachel's date has at last shown up, and Ross, no longer needed, gulps in surprise, openmouthed with shock. Not only has he lost his chance to go to the prom with Rachel, she has not even noticed his intention to do so.

Monica, heretofore unaware of her brother's teenage gallantry, sits up, exclaiming, "I can't believe you did that!" And Rachel, rising out of her seat, approaches Ross, who is standing uncomfortably near the door, the camera tracking fluidly along with her. She strides over to him, puts her hands to his chest, and kisses him, to the roars of the audience and the visible pleasure of their friends. Chandler pounds Joey on the back with his fist, Monica wipes her eyes, and Phoebe claps her chair with glee. "See?" she shouts. "He's her lobster!"

Burrows argued fiercely for the blocking of the scene, believing there was no way that Ross would not get up and head toward the door once he realized what they were going to be watching, in a fruitless attempt to maintain his pride. And having Rachel cross the apartment to kiss Ross would mask her intentions until the very last instant. Marta

Kauffman was on the set as "The One with the Prom Video" was shot and listened as the audience erupted in pleasure when Rachel kissed Ross. "That didn't suck," she thought.

Contrary to the fantasies of its fervid fan base, or the woman who had approached Kauffman on Larchmont Boulevard, the creators of *Friends* had not emerged with a fully mapped plotline for the show ready to go. They were only ever a few episodes ahead of the curve, having a broad sense of how a given season might unfold but with many of the specifics remaining to be determined in the writers' room. There was never a detailed sense of where Ross and Rachel would go once they got together, and the show seemed flummoxed about what to do with them once they were involved. Could *Friends* thrive with Ross and Rachel happily in love? And what would such a show look like?

CHAPTER 8

COULD I *BE* WEARING ANY MORE CLOTHES?

Friends and Style

John Shaffner had fond memories of his apartment at 344 West Fourteenth Street, just off Ninth Avenue, a sixth-floor walk-up he shared with his partner Joe Stewart, with transoms over the doors and panel molding on the walls. It had been the grungy, pre-gentrification, "Ford to City: Drop Dead" New York, and when Shaffner was called in to mock up a set for a New York City apartment for *Friends Like Us,* he knew immediately that he wanted to draw on those places and those experiences.

Designing a multicamera television set was much like designing the sets for a play. There were only three walls, and the absence of a fourth wall meant that everything that would have to appear in a room—doors, windows, furniture—would fill a more compressed space. Much of a set designer's work revolved around the art of visual trickery, taking an empty space and creating depth, studding the space with objects of visual interest, finding methods of crafting a foreground, middle ground, and background for actors and directors to work with.

Building a set was meant to do two things, one instantly obvious and the other not. A set had to solve all the problems introduced by the pilot, but a good set would also establish a template flexible enough to encompass an untold number of future stories, and to make the creation of those new stories as effortless and fruitful as possible.

Shaffner thought it would be true to the New York spirit to have each of the bedroom doors open directly into the main space. Shaffner placed the bathroom at the other end of the living room from the bedrooms, figuring that the path from bedroom to bathroom would allow for all manner of fruitful encounters.

Kevin Bright was also looking for a color palette that extended beyond the traditional neutral colors of most other sitcoms. No grays, beiges, or browns; Bright wanted colors that popped off the screen. Bright had recently painted his own house in vivid colors. He approached Shaffner and asked him: What did he think about trying a purple set?

The kitchen, too, was designed to have the patched-together look familiar from so many Manhattan starter apartments. Figuring that Monica was a foodie, Shaffner upgraded her stove to something a bit more elegant, but everything else stayed scruffy.

Shaffner and Stewart went to lunch with James Burrows on the Paramount lot and showed him the apartment model. Burrows approved but suggested that the apartment have a more interesting window. It might be nice to have something more visually stimulating to look at. Burrows suggested something along the lines of a skylight, and Shaffner and Stewart snuck a look at each other. A skylight might have sounded good but was instantly out of the question. How would a television show feature a window built into the roof when there was no roof to the set?

But something Burrows said nagged at Shaffner, and he began to rethink his setup. The windows were a little ordinary, and could be replaced with something a bit grander. What if, instead of a skylight, they were to feature a kind of artist's-studio window?

For the knowing architectural eye, Monica's place was meant to resemble a once-grand apartment that had been chopped into smaller pieces. Burrows particularly liked a post and beam that Shaffner had designed as a quasi-separation between the kitchen and the living room. The post and beam appealed to Burrows as a visual trim for the space, an attractive background detail that would subtly remind viewers of the space's forlorn elegance.

Shaffner took the model home and got out his watercolors. He smeared light purple paint all over the model and brought it back to the lot for Bright's perusal. Bright was pleased. He wanted something noticeably different from the flat white rectangles of most network sitcoms. TV preferred everything in shades of blue, and Bright was hoping for something that felt less interchangeable. Shaffner painted the kitchen green and turquoise, colors he believed would work well with lavender.

Having designed Rachel and Monica's apartment, Shaffner now turned his attention to the coffee-shop set. New York was often a spooky, scary place, full of unforeseen difficulties and intimidating strangers. This sitcom New York, though, was intended to be notably gentler. Hardly anyone would lock their door on a show set in a city where 1,946 people had been murdered in the past year. It was to be a New York rendered at the scale of a small town, and the coffee shop would be its town hall, meeting place, and main square. It was the centerpiece of a show intended to reclaim urban life for an affluent white demographic. This was to be their New York—carefully scrubbed clean of all grime and much of its multicultural, many-voiced variety. Shaffner asked a friend who still lived in New York to wander around downtown and take photographs of any coffee shops that looked quirky and that suggested the possibility of settling in for a long chat with a friend.

Shaffner's sets would have to be fleshed out with furniture, décor, and everything else that might be necessary to give off the impression that real people, with their own taste and their own sense of style, lived there. Set decorator Greg Grande came in to put together some boards mocking up what the apartment might look like fully dressed. Grande had worked with Kauffman and Crane on *Family Album* and had been sent the script for *Friends Like Us* when they were about to shoot their pilot. Grande met with them, and after discussing the characters in depth, they collectively came to the conclusion that they were dealing with twentysomethings with little money to spend. Grande imagined Monica as a young woman who might spend her weekends at thrift shops and garage sales, on the lookout for just the right piece for her apartment.

The coffee shop would be similarly eclectic, with a rotating array of artworks adding some visual dash to the set. Grande wanted it to feel comfortable and welcoming, a community center for a roving crew of urbanites.

In the late 1980s, Greg Grande had frequented the same coffee shop as Kauffman and Crane. He would stop in to grab some coffee at Insomnia Café and would be inspired anew each time by the fabulously quirky décor inside. When it came time to dress the set of the new show's coffee shop, Grande thought again of Insomnia Café and wanted to model the set's look on what he remembered. Grande's job was to outfit the set and make it feel like a place where its characters lived, complete with furniture, rugs, décor, kitchenware, and anything else the audience might see.

Grande had his traditional circuit of haunts he would visit when on the hunt for décor for a new show. He visited the Warner Bros. prop house and was particularly enamored of its third floor, crammed full of Empire chairs, Gothic furniture, and old phonographs. Grande was taken aback by the abundance of inspirational material here and believed that this jumble of mismatched furniture was the precise look he was in search of. The pieces Grande wound up picking out were leftovers one step away from a trip to the dumpster. The couches were ripped, the chairs were tattered, but they had a kind of disheveled beauty to them.

The network executives were appalled. Why would an NBC show meant to appeal to classy, affluent viewers display such threadbare junk? And who would drink their coffee in such a pit? Warren Littlefield reluctantly accepted the look but was disturbed by the rips in the furniture and insisted that the back of the Central Perk sofa be covered to hide the rip in the fabric. By the third episode, Grande had reupholstered the couch.

Monica's apartment would be exceptionally spacious and elegant for a young woman's home, and Grande wanted to demonstrate her taste and stylishness. Grande was a superb designer, but there was just one problem: He had never been to New York. Shaffner pulled him aside and told him that when you lived in New York and didn't have a lot of money to spare, you would go out the night before trash pickup and scour the streets. There were all manner of hidden gems to be discovered among the detritus, and any New York apartment occupied by twentysomethings would likely be a mix of street-corner finds, family heirlooms hauled out from garages and attics, and thrift-store purchases.

Grande began with the white couch, which he envisioned as being inviting and familiar, the kind of sofa that a friend would happily sink into. He had come across a black-bordered hook rug with a flowered pattern that he saw as being something Monica's grandmother might have left behind for her, along with a wood buffet that might have come out of a garage or storage unit. The dining area would be a similar mélange, with deliberately mismatched chairs and a table of the sort she might find at a Sunday swap meet.

Grande found an antique 1930s hutch that he thought would be a perfect fit for Monica, and a religious tapestry that would go right over it. At the last moment, Grande's superiors got cold feet about the tapestry, and he was left to scramble for a replacement. He flipped through a book about French circus history and came across a vintage poster of a creepy-looking child riding a horse while holding a bugle and toy clown that could make for a suitable replacement. He had the page copied and a poster-size blowup printed to occupy the wall above the hutch.

Practically every New York apartment had a solid metal door, and Shaffner had resigned himself to a visually bland slab on his set. But then he began to think about New York living once more, and was reminded of the last-minute adjustments endemic to Manhattan life. Umbrellas would be grabbed off the door for a rainstorm, or bags for a trip to the store. Shaffner threw the question to Grande, and he came back a day or two later with something different. "I was thinking of putting this on the door," Grande told Shaffner, and the art director was enormously pleased with Grande's suggestion: an empty rectangular picture frame, to be hung from a hook on the back of the door.

The frame was undoubtedly an extension of what Shaffner and Grande had come to develop as Monica's style: a quirky, tongue-in-cheek décor by turns classy and jaunty. But there was symbolic heft to this find, which would end up becoming one of the show's most iconic accent pieces.

The frame, notably, was empty. There were no pictures of parents or lovers or children fitted into its contours, nor was the frame sitting atop a table or on a shelf, where we might have naturally expected it. The place of pride where one might honor the most important people in one's life had no one inside of it. Moreover, it had been ironically subverted, removed from the piano or mantel, where it might have sat in the kind of middle-class home most of the show's characters had grown up in, and flung up against a door. The markers of middle-class achievement had been undone and remade. This was a home whose residents did not yet have anyone they had pledged their lives, and picture frames, to.

Nor, for that matter, did they have any interest, as of yet, in living in the kind of home that would make a point of inviting visitors to consider the bonds of love tying it together. This was a place where picture frames might flap in the breeze or rattle against a hastily closed door. This was a place where the fusty rules of the past—of courtship and marriage and child rearing—might be violated, or rewritten.

———————

Hairdressers everywhere were in agreement. No matter who asked, no matter how politely it was requested, they would not do it anymore. A success had become a fad, which had become a national mania, and it was time to call a halt to it. "I like to see a photo," Reny Salamon, co-owner of the Los Angeles hair salon Estilo, which had been ground zero of the phenomenon, told the *Los Angeles Times* in 1997, "as long as it isn't of Jennifer Aniston circa 1994. We're way over that cut, and we won't do it here anymore." Rebecca Eckler of the *National Post* of Canada, interviewing the show's hairstylist Richard Marin, had told Marin, "My own hairdresser said to me, 'I will cut your hair any way you want. But I refuse to give you the Jennifer Aniston cut. So don't even ask.'"

What prompted this outburst of unexpected rudeness from the hairstylists of North America? Only the most popular new hairstyle for women since Farrah Fawcett's curly blond locks swept the nation in the era of *Charlie's Angels*.

The Rachel began as an attempt to temper Jennifer Aniston's unruly hair. Aniston had approached Chris McMillan, proprietor of a well-regarded Beverly Hills salon, during the first season of *Friends*. Her hair had always been kinky and long, and she was looking for something more elegant. When *Friends* premiered, Aniston had long hair, and a handful of episodes in, McMillan started to trim it. He came up with the idea of combining partial bangs with a layered look. He would trim it at the bottom, layer it, pin it, and then use a blow-dryer to give it a smooth finish.

The result was a complex but eye-catching style that made it appear as if a stylist had grown bored at the last second with his work and decided to conjoin two different hairdos. (McMillan would later acknowledge that he was high when he created the Rachel.) The front half surrounded Aniston's face, a side part with matching half-moons of hair that ran the spectrum from blond to dirty blond to brown. Aniston would sometimes wear it with a barrette, emphasizing the girlish quality of the look, like something the most popular girl in seventh grade might wear for the first day of school.

The rear was back-combed, forming a puffy curl that ascended into a small wave before falling down to her shoulders. One could almost imagine Rachel as one of the auxiliary members of a less prominent sixties girl group, the rear portion of her hair staying dismayingly immobile as she swayed to her latest single. The result was an exceedingly careful coif that looked ever-so-slightly mussed, as if Aniston had just awoken after a brief nap in one of the chairs at Central Perk. It was a woman's look that channeled a certain youthful appeal.

Soon after Aniston debuted the look on the show, the phones at NBC began to ring regularly with requests for information about Aniston's hairstyle. McMillan began to hear from women who would gladly pay top dollar for a turn in his chair if they would come out looking like Jennifer Aniston.

Women flew from New York, from Chicago, and from Dallas to visit McMillan at his salon. "It's crazy and ridiculous and they're out of their minds," McMillan told the *Los Angeles Times* in the summer of 1995. McMillan was booked four to six weeks ahead of time, but he was not the only Los Angeles hairstylist who was suddenly spending his working hours talking about the intricacies of *Friends* episodes.

Even salons that had nothing to do with the creation of the Rachel found a hefty percentage of their work now coming from attempts to re-create it. Michael Okin told the *Times* that fifteen of the fifty visitors in a single week to his Melrose Avenue salon, Yutaka, had requested the Rachel. Forty percent of the patrons of the José Eber Salon in Beverly Hills asked for the Rachel. Stylists gladly accepted the business—at first.

The success of the Rachel was a reflection of the triumph of television over its elder sibling, the movies. Time was, people had looked to movie stars to dictate their fashion choices. The American sales of men's undershirts had famously collapsed after Clark Gable removed his button-down in 1934's Best Picture–winning *It Happened One Night* to reveal bare skin. Audrey Hepburn's fondness for the designs of Hubert de Givenchy had helped to make Givenchy a globally famous brand. Television, in comparison, was a more domestic aesthetic, inclined toward the mundane. It was a form crammed full of housewives and working stiffs in unprepossessing clothing, intentionally designed to reflect a clean-scrubbed version of white, middle-class, middle-American, middlebrow aesthetics.

The Mary Tyler Moore Show and *Moonlighting* and *Murphy Brown* had paved the way, but it was *Friends* that would serve as the culmination of a trend toward uniting television and fashion. Audiences might have been charmed by a performer's look in a favorite movie, but they would return to a favorite television show week after week. Familiarity bred a kind of hunger for imitation.

The fashion triumph of *Friends* was not solely due to the Rachel. It was a product of what *Vogue* described as "the trendiest walk-in closet in America." That closet belonged to Debra McGuire, the show's costume designer. It was crammed full of pieces from Calvin Klein, BCBG Max Azria, True Grit, and Façonnable, not to mention endless pairs of Birkenstocks and Dr. Martens. There was, *Vogue* reported after a visit to the closet, an entire wall that was "a jumble of funky, retro pocketbooks."

McGuire went in for her initial interview to be costume designer on *Friends* in an olive-green wool Versace suit jacket with hefty shoulder pads and a matching miniskirt, olive-green tights, and chocolate-brown suede Karl Lagerfeld shoes, all of which she had borrowed from a friend. At the end of the interview, Marta Kauffman turned to McGuire and told her that she loved her style and wanted to see something just like it on the show. McGuire chuckled to herself at the thought that someone else's clothes had helped her win a job as costume designer.

McGuire had been trained as an artist and had been running a jewelry company in New York when she first dabbled in costume design. For an avant-garde theater spectacle about the court of King Louis XIII, she had traveled to every store she could think of in New York, looking for white petticoats. She wound up with thousands of petticoats, purchased for ten cents apiece, and a sense of the combination of artistry and mass production that was costume design.

A studio executive in Los Angeles had suggested she come west to see what film work might interest her, and after a PA stint on the Steve

Martin film *My Blue Heaven*, she had fallen into a gig as a costume designer on network movies of the week. McGuire struggled with a sense of disbelief at the entertainment industry. Were people genuinely earning a living for doing this? It seemed far too amusing to be paid work.

When McGuire was hired for *Friends*, she made an effort to differentiate its six protagonists by giving each of them a look of their own. Television, McGuire thought, was a two-dimensional medium and could be approached like a painting. It was all a matter of color and texture, and working in tandem with Greg Grande and John Shaffner, the screen could be decorated like a palette.

Marta Kauffman's initial impulse was to dress the show's characters in jeans and move on. It would be a nod to realism—what more could these characters afford?—and to her own New York life. McGuire insisted otherwise.

McGuire had spent much of the 1980s living in Japan, and what little she had seen of American television had offended her sensibilities. Everything was so drab and careful, designed not to stand out in any way. McGuire was looking to do something notably different. It was her idea that the clothing the show's characters wore should be aspirational. McGuire wanted her characters to look glamorous more than she cared about their realistically portraying twentysomething style.

For the pilot, McGuire had less than one week to dress her characters, and she searched the costume department at Warner Bros. for a wedding dress to introduce Rachel. McGuire's daughter had been born on a Thursday, and on the following Monday morning, she was toting her around in a basket as she browsed the racks. She discovered a creamy, lacy confection that she thought might be perfect for a spoiled Long Island girl mapping out her dream wedding. (It would also show off Aniston's shoulders to maximal effect.)

Each character was assigned their own color and their own place on the preppy-to-hippie spectrum. The show was like a tableau, and McGuire wanted to dress the characters so that no matter who might be in a given scene, there would be an ebb and flow of patterns and colors and styles.

Chandler would regularly wear sweater vests, along with a black button-down with a gray racing stripe that would come to be his early-season calling card. The shirt reminded McGuire of ones her father had worn when she was a child and had some of the retro flair she was hoping to associate with the show's look. Joey was intended to be soft and huggable in sweaters, a deliberate reaction to the leather-jacketed player of the pilot. Ross would be dressed in corduroys and tweeds.

The female characters were distinguished by their preferred colors. Rachel went with greens and blues; Monica leaned toward red, black, and gray. Phoebe preferred yellows and purples, mixed patterns, skirts, and unstructured pieces.

The clothing was meant to be an essential part of the story, subtly reflecting the script. When Monica was unemployed, her clothing selections were intended to reflect both her diminished circumstances and her no longer needing to dress daily for work. The look was meant to be emulatable.

At the start, McGuire made a significant portion of the clothing her characters would wear. Handcrafted clothing required numerous fittings to get the tailoring right, and as the show progressed, and the demands on the actors' time swelled, the actors balked at the additional work required of them. In later seasons, McGuire would only make special items, like wedding dresses; everything else would be off-the-rack.

She was invested in each of her characters' looks, but the audience established its preferences early on. The boys were handsomely dressed but visually dull, and while Phoebe and Monica were appealing, it was Rachel Green who captivated a nation of young women looking for inspiration about what it meant to dress themselves fashionably. Only Rachel would eventually inspire Internet scholars to document and rank each of the 703 outfits she wore over *Friends'* ten seasons.

Why were fans so captivated by Rachel's looks? Aniston was

beautiful, to be sure, and, playing a fashionable character, was more likely to dress herself stylishly than her compatriots. But the fascination with Rachel's look also spoke to something at the core of *Friends'* appeal: its service as a manual to adulthood.

Rachel was a role model for the aspiring adults of Generation X. Her life might occasionally have been a mess, her romantic instincts sometimes misguided, but she never looked anything less than stunning along the way. At times, Rachel came perilously close to the movie stereotype of the beautiful woman whose humanizing flaw is her relentless klutziness, but she was more than that. Rachel was our down-home Audrey Hepburn, our entry-level Grace Kelly.

McGuire's preference for rarely repeating an outfit emphasized a latent belief of *Friends*, and a part of its fashion allure: the notion that there was a right outfit for every occasion. The show may have begun as a portrait of postcollegiate "welcome to the real world" ennui, but it rapidly shifted gears toward encroaching maturity, and the clothing choices followed behind. We watched Rachel to see what we might look like as a woman in the workforce, or a woman in love, or a new mother, or a woman scorned, or a woman with a killer new job. To do so was to glance into a highly flattering mirror that showed us only from the right angle, in the right light.

Marta Kauffman was invested in the selection of clothing for the show, and one of McGuire's weekly tasks was to oversee the "rack check," in which Kauffman ran through all the different costumes selected for the next episode. Kauffman generally approved of McGuire's taste, but there were times when Kauffman worried that a particular outfit might be too distracting, pulling viewers' attention away from the dialogue, and so a standout item might be replaced by something a bit more demure.

Friends stuck fairly rigorously to a predetermined color palette for each character, and so it surprised McGuire when the actors approached her with last-minute requests. If something felt too tight or seemed unsuitable, they might ask for a replacement and wonder why they couldn't wear something in black. McGuire, mentally wielding her carefully designed color fields, would point out that Monica was wearing black in the scene.

She realized that even late in the show's run, the actors remained blissfully unaware of the thought that had gone into the costume design. This was, perhaps, how it was intended to be; with few exceptions, and other than for the most carefully trained eye, the costumes were merely another silent expression of the characters' personalities.

McGuire and her team would visit thrift stores and consignment shops and mass-market retailers and designer emporiums in search of inspiration. Merely providing dozens of new costumes for *Friends'* characters every week was an enormous undertaking.

One notable, and entertaining, exception to the profusion of styles came with "The One Where No One's Ready," from the third season. Ross's anxiety over shepherding his friends out the door for a work event spilled over into a dispute between Joey and Chandler. An escalating series of schemes leads to Chandler's disposing of all of Joey's underwear, forcing him to wear a rented tuxedo with nothing of his own to serve as protection. Joey swears revenge and comes back wearing all of Chandler's clothes—and still without underwear.

McGuire and her colleagues took everything from Chandler's wardrobe and stitched together a Frankenstein's-monster costume, layering the pieces until they were satisfied with the final result. Then they sewed it all together until it had become a kind of two-piece LeBlanc could step into. It was a quick change, coming as it did in the middle of a scene, and their stitch job made it a cinch for LeBlanc to pull off a hilarious adjustment.

Friends was such a fashion phenomenon that fans would even take it upon themselves to request items they had only glimpsed. For "The One with the Lesbian Wedding," McGuire had designed a wedding dress for Carol to wear. It was made from cream-colored raw silk, with a striking off-the-shoulder design that accentuated Jane Sibbett's long, elegant neck. After the show aired, McGuire began getting calls from women hoping to order the wedding dress she had designed. McGuire worked with one bride who would fly in from Boston for dress fittings. *Friends* helped to make McGuire the kind of designer who could charge upward of $6,000 for a wedding gown and as much as $3,500 for a suit.

Her growing reputation helped McGuire to open her own shop in Pacific Palisades and start her own fashion line. She designed Lisa Kudrow's wedding dress, another off-the-shoulder number made from ivory satin, and the lavender dress Courteney Cox wore to the Emmys in 1995. The red-carpet business dried up once designers began offering their gowns free of charge, so McGuire transitioned to making clothing for directors and directors' spouses for awards shows. She also made Marta Kauffman's wardrobe for fund-raisers and other events.

McGuire was terribly dismayed when a *Vogue* profile of her in 1996 included unflattering references by the author to Kudrow, implying that her figure was dumpier and more in need of being covered up than the more sylphlike Cox and Aniston. Kudrow was stung by the mention, and her fellow actors rallied to her side in support. McGuire's relationship with the performers she dressed was never quite the same afterward, even though she had not been the one to make the nasty remark about Kudrow.

In season 2 and beyond, we knew *Friends'* characters were growing up because we watched them dress more maturely, more sensibly, more like the adults they were becoming. Rachel in particular went from unemployed former future housewife to coffee-shop waitress to fashion-company employee. Fashion entered the lexicon of the show itself, with Rachel working at Bloomingdale's, then Ralph Lauren. McGuire knew she had to feature some Ralph Lauren clothing—it was called for in the script—but preferred to limit their exposure on the show. It was important to her that *Friends* not become a show that was exclusively outfitted by any one designer. McGuire still wanted Rachel to be able to look alluring and sexy but preferred a wardrobe that a working woman in her twenties might enjoy having. *Friends* intended to make the experience of being young and driftless a universal one, and essential to that process was the desire to visually demonstrate the process of encroaching maturity.

The Rachel eventually gave way to other hairstyles, another outfit in the closet of *Friends'* discarded looks. Even as the show moved on, intent on keeping its style forever fresh, women continued showing up at salons asking to be remade as Rachel Green. *Friends'* success had spilled off the television screen and into the world at large. The show was more than a hit; it was now a phenomenon. Instead of seeking to reflect the world back to its viewers, it had remade the world after its own image. Everywhere you went, there was *Friends*.

CHAPTER 9

WE WERE ON A BREAK

The Ballad of Ross and Rachel, Part 2

The writers worked out a superlatively dirty joke for Ross and Rachel's first time having sex in the second season's "The One Where Ross and Rachel . . . You Know" that belied some of the showrunners' repeated complaints about *Friends'* being prevented from telling the kinds of jokes they were getting away with on *Seinfeld*. Ross invites Rachel to his job at the Museum of Prehistoric History (a stand-in for the Museum of Natural History), animal-skin blanket and juice boxes in hand, and shows her the (surprisingly dim) stars. (Kevin Bright was terribly disappointed with how the light-show sequence turned out, complaining so bitterly about the botched job that producer Todd Stevens momentarily worried he might lose his job over it.) As they begin taking off their clothes and rolling around on the floor, Rachel pauses and comforts Ross, telling him it's no big deal. Ross pauses, momentarily confused, and then tells her, "Oh, no. You just rolled over the juice box."

Much like *Seinfeld's* "The Contest," an extended joke about jerking off that never used the word *masturbate*, *Friends* was getting away with a joke about premature ejaculation by a careful elision of giveaway words. It might be the moment, or it might merely be good acting, but Aniston and Schwimmer feel as if they are laughing for real here, swept up in their characters' sense of relief at momentary sexual disaster averted. Later, David Crane was convinced that writer Greg Malins had come up with the joke, while Malins was sure it was Mike Sikowitz, and Sikowitz was positive it was Crane. This was symbolic of the writing process on the show, where no one could or would take credit for a classic joke.

There were obvious markers to reach—first kiss, first time having sex—and *Friends* did them well and humorously, but Ross and Rachel's relationship never really settled into a period of calm. Even in its earliest moments, there were intimations that the romantically inept Ross was going to be surprisingly controlling and forbidding. In "The One Where Joey Moves Out," he hectors Rachel about having gotten a tattoo, before considering the possibilities and softening: "Is it sore, or can ya . . . do stuff?" The thought of her "meaningless animal sex," as Rachel calls it, with her ex-boyfriend Paolo (admittedly, an infelicitous phrase to use with your current boyfriend) drives him to distraction.

Ross unspools an entire plan for their future, complete with two children (one boy and one girl) and a home in Scarsdale, so they can be far enough from their parents to breathe but close enough to call on them to babysit. "One minute, I'm holding Ben like a football," Rachel complains, referring to Ross's son, "the next thing I know, I've got two kids, I'm living in Scarsdale, complaining about the taxes!" Ross agrees to slow his roll, enjoying the relationship for what it is and not what he intends it to be, but their burgeoning romance is poisoned by Ross's creeping jealousy.

Needy and insecure, Ross is the high school geek who still cannot believe that a beautiful woman might give him the time of day and is transformed into a sexist stereotype by his insecurity. Ross is instantly jealous when he hears about someone who might offer Rachel a job: "Sounds like Mark something wants to have some sex."

"Don't you trust her?" Monica asks her brother, attempting to slap some sense into him. "Then get over yourself. Grow up!"

Monica's intercession is unsuccessful, for Ross remains every bit as distrustful once Rachel starts her new job. He calls her at work, accusatory: "What's Mark doing answering your phone?" Ross is called on the carpet for his flagrant misbehavior, and he acknowledges his weaknesses. Still reeling from the loss of his ex-wife, he is apprehensive someone will take Rachel away from him, just as Carol was taken. (Central Perk barista Gunther, eavesdropping on the conversation, mumbles his own incantation: "Let it be me, let it be me.")

By the middle of the third season, Ross has toppled over into outright hostility toward Rachel's non-Ross-related pursuits. Ross is strangely resentful of Rachel's career ambitions. He was once critical of her being "just a waitress," but when she finds professional purpose, he calls it "just a job."

Ross is a good friend but a bad boyfriend, and after winning Rachel over, he begins to take her for granted. Ross's low point comes when he invades Rachel's office at a stressful moment during the workday in "The One Where Ross and Rachel Take a Break," lighting candles for a lavish lunch spread as Rachel silently fumes. ("Excuse me," she tells a caller, "I'm going to have to call you back. I've got Shemp in my office.") "I don't feel like I even have a girlfriend anymore," Ross whines, and Rachel, drained, later suggests that they take "a break from us."

Ross famously misinterprets Rachel's suggestion, first thinking she means they should get frozen yogurt and then believing he is a sexual free agent. Ross calls that evening and hears that Mark is at her apartment, and heads out to a party, where he is yanked onto the dance floor by lovely copy-shop employee Chloe (Angela Featherstone), whom Joey and Chandler have been semi-creepily enthusing about for much of the season.

There is a clever, subtle callback here to the beginning of Ross and Rachel's romance, with U2's "With or Without You" playing when Chloe gets Ross to dance with her. "I like this song," Ross mutters, and viewers may remember that Ross dedicated this very song to Rachel over the radio when seeking to apologize for his callous pros-and-cons behavior the previous season. Even in his moment of forgetting Rachel, some part of Ross is reminded of her.

In truth, the writing staff had hit a wall and realized that coupling up Ross and Rachel might have been emotionally satisfying for the audience, but it was destroying their narrative momentum. Kauffman and Crane had known from the outset that they would have to split up Ross and Rachel. It was just a matter of when. Without the engine of Ross and Rachel's longing, the show was in danger of becoming fatally bland.

"We were on a break!" soon became one of *Friends'* trustiest punch lines, revisited and resuscitated numerous times over the course of the show, but "The One with the Morning After" is actually among the rawest, most emotional episodes of the series. Rachel, her moment of pique having passed, was trying to call Ross while he was about to sleep with Chloe, and the next morning, she stops by his apartment as he attempts to hide her from sight. Ross feels guilty and plans to confess, but Chandler talks him out of it: "At least wait until the timing's right. And that's what deathbeds are for."

Rachel finds out and is furious with Ross for his presumption and his cruelty. She trains the intensity of her gaze on Ross's inadequacies, and her boyfriend withers under the laser beam of her contempt. "A mistake?" she echoes, parroting his sad excuse for his behavior. "What were you trying to put it in, her purse?" Their friends are trapped in Monica's bedroom as Ross and Rachel vainly attempt to work it out, eavesdropping on the death throes of their romance.

Ross and Rachel's friends serve as a surrogate audience to their dispute, their hopes and fears channeling the audience's own. "They're going to get through this, aren't they?" wonders Phoebe.

"Yeah, come on, it's Ross and Rachel," answers Chandler. "They've got to."

"What if they don't?" asks Monica.

There is an unstated understanding that even this will be overcome, the show's triumphant romance upheld at all costs, but this is a decoy. Ross and Rachel will not work things out, and their break will become permanent. "This can't be it," Ross tells Rachel, to which she replies, "Then how come it is?" The camera pulls out on their standing still in Rachel's living room, frozen in the realization that there is nothing left to say.

CHAPTER 10

HOW MANY CAMERAS ARE ACTUALLY ON YOU?

Contract Negotiations

David Schwimmer, as the first breakout star from the show, was also the first to be approached about reupping his contract for the third season in 1996. NBC executives expected some challenges but figured Schwimmer would be more than happy to reap a financial windfall from the most successful television series of its time. What they did not bank on was David Schwimmer.

Schwimmer's mother, Arlene Coleman-Schwimmer, was a successful divorce lawyer, and young David had grown up in a house where discussions of fair allocations of assets were dinner-table talk. Moreover, after attending Northwestern University, Schwimmer had founded the Lookingglass Theatre Company in Chicago. The Lookingglass was an artistic collective in which resources were shared, and the notion of one actor's being paid more than another was anathema. At Lookingglass, no one made enough to support themselves—the actors were all holding down second jobs to get by—but each actor was paid the same. Good theater came out of a sense of community, and *Friends* was not only a hit television show; it was a theatrical ensemble, in which six performers would have to work together, week in and week out, on new plays. Schwimmer was pushing for his costars to think of themselves as "a union of the six of [them]."

Schwimmer knew that each of his costars had signed a different contract (although they all ran the same five years). He also knew that he was neither the highest-paid actor on the show nor the lowest-paid one. "OK, I'm being advised to go in for more money," he later told Warren Littlefield about his thought process at the time. "But for me, it goes against everything I truly believe in, in terms of ensemble. The six of us are all leads on the show. We are all here for the same amount of hours. The story lines are always balanced."

Schwimmer was emboldened by Warner Bros.' audacity in publicly bragging about the windfall profits that were due to them for *Friends'* syndication rights. The studio was sharing its belief that in two years' time, when *Friends* was eligible for syndication, it would receive around $4 million per episode for approximately ninety episodes—an enormous windfall. Merely the first two seasons alone would garner $192 million in syndication payments. How could it make sense for Warner Bros. and the show's creators to reap hundreds of millions of dollars from *Friends'* success while its stars were left with so little in comparison?

Now Schwimmer was being offered the financial comfort that was many actors' dream, and he hesitated, thinking of his costars. How could he sit at the rehearsal table, working with his friends and colleagues, knowing that he had gotten a lucrative payday and they had not? So Schwimmer approached his costars and did the unthinkable: He asked them to talk about their salaries.

"Here's the deal," he told them. "I'm being advised to ask for more money, but I think, instead of that, we should all go in together. There's this expectation that I'm going in to ask for a pay raise. I think we should use this opportunity to talk openly about the six of us being paid the same." He suggested they threaten to walk off the set if their demands were not met.

When *Friends* was being cast, none of the show's performers, with the exception of Courteney Cox, had prior hits, and even Cox was not truly a bona fide star yet. But after two seasons, the six stars of *Friends* held similarly lofty places in the Hollywood firmament, with each the subject of unending professional, romantic, and personal speculation. And yet, given the realities of television acting and the pay scale, they were being paid notably different salaries for what amounted to the same work. Each actor had signed a five-year contract, locking them in at what was now a criminally low rate (beginning at $22,500 per episode) for performers who were regularly splashed across magazine front covers and whose show dominated the weekly Nielsen ratings, coming in eighth place for the 1994–95 season and third in 1995–96. (By comparison, the supporting cast of *Seinfeld* were receiving $150,000 per episode, soon to be quadrupled to $600,000.)

In making the argument, Schwimmer had the benefit of the show's own structure and balance on his side. *Friends* was a show with six equal costars. Lines and plots were parceled out equally to each of the performers, so how could it make sense for them to be paid differing amounts for the same work? Coleman-Schwimmer treated her son's costars like so many jilted spouses, insisting they know the value of their labor and suggesting that they negotiate in unison. They agreed to ask for $100,000 per episode, which would more than double the highest previous salary for any actor on the show.

Warner Bros. had a history of stonewalling what it perceived to be excessive contract demands. In addition, the failure of cinematic vehicles like *The Pallbearer* and *Ed* rendered the stars' supposed feature-film bankability substantially more precarious than it might previously have been assumed to be.

Friends was still in the early flush of its success, and there was little doubt that everyone wanted the show to return for a fourth season. It was fairly common practice for networks to offer early contract extensions to simultaneously reward their stars and keep a show's key players locked in. NBC countered with an offer of $80,000 per episode for the following seasons. Even though Schwimmer (and his mother) had guided the negotiation process, the show's stars felt the need to deny that any one actor was leading the charge. This was undoubtedly out of a desire to avoid singling anyone out as responsible for their demands but also spoke to their preference for equality in all things.

Matthew Perry later told *Entertainment Weekly* that Schwimmer had never threatened to leave the show without a raise: "It was the year to renegotiate and we thought it was best for the dynamic of the show if we did it together. We didn't want one person making a fortune and someone else making nothing. Public perception of us changed a little because of it, I think, and that's not good."

The enormous numbers under discussion transformed the *Friends* cast into another example in the ongoing national fascination with, and panic over, excess pay. The negotiation was going on just two years after Major League Baseball had canceled its World Series for the first time ever, with players on strike for a more generous labor deal and owners fearful about overpaying stars in free agency. It was also a moment in which the media was fretfully reporting about movie stars like Jim Carrey cracking the $20-million-per-film barrier. Americans loved a success story, and also loved to complain about out-of-touch elites and their excessive salaries.

It would have been possible for Schwimmer, or Jennifer Aniston, to do better if they negotiated alone, but the results spoke for themselves. After a five-hour late-night session, the union of six walked away with a new four-year deal that began with a collective salary bump to $75,000 per episode starting with the third season. The new contract included a salary increase for each forthcoming season, with $85,000 for the fourth season, $100,000 for the fifth, and $125,000 for the sixth. The numbers were substantial, but the joint deal also meant that each *Friends* star was now being paid as well as the lowest-paid cast member would have been.

The deal also gave Warner Bros. and NBC an additional guaranteed year of *Friends*, with the initial five-year contract now replaced by one that included a sixth season as well. The show was clearly going to continue beyond its first five years, and so purchasing a sixth season—even at a cost of $18 million for just above-the-line acting talent—was well worth it. An additional year of syndication rights alone would be worth, by Warner Bros.' calculations, $100 million.

Meanwhile, the creators of *Friends* were being offered their own opportunities for enrichment—and they were intent on grabbing them. This, they were told, was the next step. If you had a hit television show, the logical play—the *only* play—was to produce another show, and another, and another, until you ran a mini-empire of smash hits. After three seasons of *Friends,* the show appeared to be a well-oiled machine that would only require occasional maintenance to keep running indefinitely. Crane and Kauffman's representatives pushed them to branch out and start up a new series for NBC. The network was hungry for more original material from them, hoping to offset the likely impending disappearance of *Seinfeld* and *Mad About You* with some new smash hits.

The two writers went off and came back with a proposal for a series about a romance expert whose own romantic life comes crashing down to earth when her husband leaves her. *Friends* had been cunningly modeled on *Cheers,* and so Kauffman and Crane's next show would seek to borrow some of *Cheers's* fairy dust by casting none other than Kirstie Alley.

The combination of Bright/Kauffman/Crane Productions' savvy comedic instincts and the star wattage of Alley fairly guaranteed another smash hit for NBC, and *Veronica's Closet* debuted in the fall of 1997 in the prime slot immediately following *Seinfeld.*

For David Crane, being a budding mogul meant not doing the thing he was best at in the world so he could play a role he did not particularly want to play. Crane was instructed to delegate the work of *Friends* to others while he devoted himself to getting *Veronica's Closet* off the ground. Crane found that he was continually leaving rooms in which he wanted to stay in order to enter rooms he did not particularly want to be in.

"Why are you doing this?" his partner, Jeffrey Klarik, asked him. "You're so happy. Why are you doing this?" Crane could not come up with a suitable answer, other than "I'm supposed to."

Crane would pull off the same trick in both rooms, entering and listening quietly as a particular joke or story point was the subject of ardent debate. When the conversation reached a temporary lull, Crane would weave together the differing strands of ideas into one perfectly taut and pleasing rope of plot. Heads would nod at this remarkable feat of writerly ingenuity. Then he would leave, and the writers would collectively panic: Had anyone written all of that down?

It would have been a manageable difficulty if it had only been Crane who preferred his firstborn to his newborn, but Kauffman and Bright also found that they preferred *Friends* to *Veronica's Closet*. Crane and Kauffman drove the writers just as hard in the *Veronica's Closet* room as they did for *Friends*. And many of the writers had either already written for *Friends* or would go on to do so. As much of themselves as they poured into *Veronica's Closet*, they never cracked the code of what the show was to be about or who it was for. The best team of writers in the world could not do that work for them, and so *Veronica's Closet* floundered.

Friends had rapidly come to understand what it was best at, and *Veronica's Closet*, stuffed full of potential, could not manage the same trick. It was, ultimately, less about what went wrong with *Veronica's Closet* and more about what had gone right with *Friends*. It simply did not matter how many talented, hardworking, brilliant people you might gather together; creating great television was at least partially a matter of blind luck. *Veronica's Closet*, writer Ellen Kreamer (who would soon go on to work on *Friends*) thought, suffered from never entirely being able to figure out just what it was.

Matters only got worse with the premiere of *Jesse* the following season. *Friends* veteran Ira Ungerleider created the show, starring Christina

Applegate as a single mother juggling a new boyfriend, a newly returned ex-husband, and a cranky father whose bar she worked at. The general consensus was that if Crane and Kauffman were able to devote themselves to *Veronica's Closet* with the same tenacity they gave to *Friends*, it could be a solid piece of television comedy. Kevin Bright believed *Jesse* lacked that potential, even with Kauffman and Crane's involvement, and that it had been a mistake to empower an idea they had not originated, especially one that he saw as being worse than mediocre.

Veronica's Closet lasted three seasons; *Jesse* only made it two. The promise of a future Bright/Kauffman/Crane empire had fizzled unceremoniously, and David Crane, for one, could not have been any more pleased about it. The truth was, the life of the television mogul was not for him. Crane understood that he was not meant to be a supervisor. Other showrunners could transform into superintendents, overseeing others' writing, but the contracting of Crane's world felt nothing short of wonderful. Nothing could distract him now from the business of writing *Friends*.

CHAPTER 11

THE FIFTH DENTIST

Long Days and Longer Nights Inside the Writers' Room

Every writer knew the sinking feeling in the pit of their stomach. David Crane would enter the room, toting a script full of notes scribbled in the margins. He would sit down in his chair and begin drumming his fingers on the table before announcing, "All right, we've got a lot of really good stuff here." The assembled writers would silently groan, knowing that this was Crane-ian code for a full script rewrite. Everything was out, and it was time to start again.

"Good enough" was not a concept Crane, or Marta Kauffman, understood or accepted. One day during the first season, writer Jeff Astrof approached Crane with a proposal. "Look," he told Crane, "right now we work one hundred percent of the allotted time and we have a show that's one hundred. I believe that if we worked fifty percent of the time we'd have a show that's seventy-five, so maybe we work seventy-five percent of the time and have a show that's like a ninety." Crane instantly rejected the proposal: "Absolutely not. The show has to be one hundred." There might have been a faster way to get the work done. But this was Marta Kauffman and David Crane's show, and their room.

After hiring their staff for the first season, Crane and Kauffman gathered the writers to deliver a pep talk, and a challenge. "Comedy is king," Crane told the assembled writers. "This is a show where we want everything to be as funny as it can be." For writers in their midtwenties, many of whom were on their first or second jobs in the industry, this was a thrilling proclamation. Writers like the team of Astrof and Mike Sikowitz had always felt deeply competitive about crafting the best possible joke and getting it into the script—Astrof's concerns about the punishing schedule notwithstanding—and Crane was seemingly opening the doors wide to all competitors.

Sikowitz soon realized that Kauffman and Crane felt confident about being able to supply the emotional backbone for the show, leading the process of designing the season-long arcs for each character, and were counting on their writing staff to jam their scripts full of as many killer jokes as possible. It was a remarkable feeling to be given the green light to simply be funny. The planning of emotional beats was a major part of the preparatory work for the season and would be done by the writers' room as a whole, but it was understood that Kauffman and Crane were the ablest writers when it came to finding the nuances of feeling that would hook viewers.

The *Friends* writers' room was simultaneously a party room and a prison cell, a wild daily gathering whose participants, like the dinner guests in Luis Buñuel's *The Exterminating Angel*, could never leave. Participants were thrilled to be a part of the work of writing *Friends*. Each day was a marvel, and it was an honor to be granted the opportunity to work alongside such gifted, committed, fiercely original imaginations. But it was simply not possible to avoid occasionally sighing and wishing to go home.

Adam Chase was astounded by the regular fourteen-to-sixteen-hour days around the giant desk in the seventh-floor boardroom, which on occasion stretched to a full twenty-four-hour shift, like a doctor on call or a factory worker earning overtime pay. But for Chase, the drudgery was also a moveable feast, an ongoing party that he was lucky enough to be invited to on a daily basis. A good deal of the pleasure came from Crane and Kauffman's willingness to let relative newcomers like Chase play as near-equals.

On many shows, there was one overhanging question lingering behind any discussion in the writers' room: "What's the pitch?" If you weren't coming in with a distinct, carefully worked-out resolution to the problem you were chewing over, there simply was no time to devote to your musings. The showrunner would be annoyed at your having wasted their time, and the conversation would rapidly move on to more fertile territory.

This was never how *Friends* worked. Crane and Kauffman were only too pleased to have any one of their writers, however young or inexperienced, bring the discussion to a halt with a question or concern. Kauffman and Crane would listen and then open it up to the room. How do we solve this problem?

This was in part because Crane and Kauffman themselves were still relatively new to the ways of television. They had never been writers in someone else's room, having gone directly from theater to freelancing to running *Dream On*. Crane, by his own estimation, lacked time-management skills, content to let his staff wander far afield before returning to the task at hand.

The remarkable thing about the *Friends* writers' room, Chase believed, was its complete allergy to compromise. Not only would Kauffman and Crane never admit defeat and accept what they deemed a mediocre line or joke, neither would any of the members of their staff. (On one rare occasion, after an exceedingly poor run-through, Crane had asked NBC if they might skip that week's episode. NBC said they would take a new episode in whatever shape it was in, and "The One Where Rachel Smokes" proceeded to air.)

Friends' style was adapted from *Seinfeld's* interlocked model, in which each episode had an A, B, and C plot (Carol is pregnant; Monica is cooking for her parents; Rachel has misplaced her engagement ring). This created the challenge of intertwining separate stories, but it also prompted an insatiable hunger for story lines. A single season of *Friends* would require seventy-two separate plots, each with its own introduction and resolution, each with its own array of jokes and emotional moments. And fully plotted stories would regularly be tossed out because they flopped in rehearsals or during a shoot. The sheer volume of polished material that the writers of *Friends* had to come up with placed inordinate pressure on the writers' room to work in sync and to pick up each other's slack.

On other shows, more emphasis would be placed on individual effort. Writers would go off on their own and craft scripts, and while the room might polish them, they would remain demonstrably the product of an individual's effort. *Friends* was different. Writers would write the first drafts and ultimately be granted credit for the episode. But the true work was done in the room, together. Everyone was responsible for improving each line, each joke, each emotional beat of the show, and it would never be enough to simply do your own work.

Writers would have to endure the process of watching their scripts be slowly, steadily dismantled and rebuilt. To bristle at the process, or to attempt to defend a rejected joke, was counterproductive and would reflect poorly on the writer who attempted it. Writers soon learned that it was far better to jump in and help fix your own script than attempt to protect your original work. This was a team, and anyone who insisted on publicly totting up their batting average would soon find themselves riding the end of the bench. (Later in the show's run, there were joke rubber stamps passed out to the staff that read, "I Pitched That!")

The *Friends* writers' room was, as some of its participants described it, a remarkable feat of alchemy, in which a dozen talented individuals transformed into a team that was far greater than the sum of its parts. Crane and Kauffman were responsible for hiring writers who each had their own preferred writing style and voice, and ensuring that they complemented each other. It was like an arranged marriage between a dozen different people, and should have been as impossible. Instead, there was a kind of magic present in the room, where writers competing to tell the best joke were also able to carve out their own voices.

Sitting at opposite ends of the conference-room table, Kauffman and Crane were curators of the staff's efforts. Rather than looking for a fully formed idea that could be inserted directly into the script, they were happy to gather the shards of their writers' inspiration. They would take one idea from here and one joke from there, and begin assembling workable material. And if they hadn't found something they were pleased with, they would tell the writers to keep looking. Their writers' lack of experience was a bonus, not a problem. More than anything, Crane and Kauffman did not want to hear from their writers that this was the way it had always been done on *Who's the Boss?* They preferred the company of young writers who did not know about How It Was Done on Television.

The result was an atmosphere that was simultaneously competitive and cooperative. Mike Sikowitz would have times when he drove home to West Hollywood after a long day on the Burbank lot with a feeling of intense disappointment over not having managed to get a single solid joke into the script that day. "What's wrong with me?" he would think. "I used to be funny." On the days where Sikowitz successfully logged some killer jokes, he would make the same drive home feeling like he was the king of the world. Being in the *Friends* writers' room, Sikowitz thought, was like an emotional stock market. Some days you made a killing, and others you lost your shirt.

It was fun to be in a room of raconteurs, entertainers, and one-liner machines bantering, debating, and performing for each other. But there also was no specified end to the workday, no moment when the writers would punch out and head home. Ordering dinner at the office was a matter of course. All-nighters were a fairly standard occurrence. On David Lagana's first day on the job as a writers' assistant, he showed up for work at nine thirty A.M. and left for home at six forty-five the next morning. The last day of the workweek was widely known as Fraturday, as it often did not end until Saturday morning. "I think I just saw your beard grow," Alexa Junge told Mike Sikowitz during one late night.

The writers would entertain themselves with antics like tossing a small toy football back and forth for hours without letting it drop (which would inspire the episode "The One with the Ball") or offering cash inducements to eat an entire jar of garlic pickles. They would play video games to blow off steam or watch the latest installment of *The Osbournes*. And then there were Taste Test Wednesdays, when Scott Silveri or one of the other showrunners would send an assistant to the grocery store to purchase, say, every brand of plain potato chip. The writers would try each variety and vote on their favorites, and then the singular best potato chip would be declared, to the merriment of the assembled judges.

On days when it became clear that it would be another late night, the writers would put on their preferred jam, Chuck Mangione's jazz-fusion hit "Feels So Good," on their boombox and listen to it as the sun went down. Sometimes, their dinner order would arrive at the same time, and the writers would burst into Mangione-inspired song: "The food is here, the food is here." It was no surprise, given what passed for entertainment there, that the room transformed everyone, as Ellen Kreamer thought, into a slightly fatter, greasier-looking version of themselves. Even years later, Kreamer would find that the sound of a crinkling takeout bag would be enough to bring her momentary joy.

One late night, writer Shana Goldberg-Meehan, who joined the show in the fourth season, entered the room, took note of the roiling discontent, and told fellow writers Kreamer and Robert Carlock that they had thirty seconds to go "apeshit crazy" before they got back to work. Kreamer and Carlock jumped on tables and tore the room apart for precisely thirty seconds. It was also the late nights when the conversation in the room, fueled by boredom and exhaustion, often turned to its bawdiest and most puerile, for which there would be notable long-term consequences.

On the rare evenings when he was able to leave the office early

(early for *Friends*, about ten thirty P.M.), Adam Chase would get home, smoke some weed, and turn on the eleven P.M. rerun of *Law & Order*. Working on *Friends* was so intense that Chase needed some time to decompress at the end of the day, but he found that his mind was still coming up with jokes—only now they were for Jerry Orbach's Detective Lennie Briscoe.

Chase was later introduced to René Balcer, a *Law & Order* producer, who suggested Chase try his hand at some punch-ups for their jokes. In one, Briscoe was talking to a medical examiner standing next to a body with a javelin sticking out of its chest. "What made you go into this line of work?" Briscoe asked. The best the *Law & Order* crew could come up with was "To meet charming detectives like you." Chase, whose comic sensibility had been forged in the fires of *Friends*, knew he had a better answer: "Free javelins."

Jeff Astrof would look out through the room's wall of windows during the endless days working over scripts in the first season, and watch sets being built for the Michael Jordan–starring Looney Tunes film *Space Jam* (1996). He was surprised to find himself staring at the construction workers and thinking to himself, "Now, that's a cool job." There was a profession in which one's progress could be assessed on a daily basis, in which there were no notes or comments from one's superiors. At the end of one's labors, there was a physical object that had not existed prior to the start of one's work. The idea of a working life without a constant stream of notes and suggestions and rewrites was deeply tempting to Astrof.

Astrof would joke that, on those regular early-morning drives home, he would encounter himself returning to the office, ripping a hole in the space-time continuum. Crane would regularly endure the deeply unpleasant experience of driving home from the Valley to Brentwood during the A.M. rush hour, making what would normally be an easy reverse commute into a harrowing drive. Crane would find himself drifting off to sleep at red lights and resorted to calling his partner, Jeffrey Klarik, on his car phone and demanding that he chat with him in order to keep him awake on the drive home. Writers would learn what it looked like to see the sun come up over the Warner Bros. lot.

Kauffman, who had two young children, particularly feared having a story collapse during run-through, since this would inevitably lead to another very late night. Kauffman had a private rule: She would not miss her children's bedtime two nights in a row. On late nights, Kauffman would drive home, put her children to bed, and then return to the office. On *very* late nights, Kauffman would drive home as the sun came up, shower, feed her children breakfast and get them dressed for school, and head back to work.

Sometimes, the best jokes would emerge out of the late-late-night sessions, when writers were sagging in their chairs or napping on one of the couches. They would be staring out the windows as days turned into nights, and the glimpses of the world going on without them on the streets below would be transformed, with the sun's departure, into a mirror reflecting their own faces back at them.

Exhaustion had the propensity to tear away the expected response and sometimes reveal the odder pitch lurking underneath. One late night during the first season, the staff was talking through the episode "The One Where the Monkey Gets Away," in which Rachel accidentally allows Ross's monkey, Marcel, to escape and everyone fans out to search for him.

There was a scene in which Joey and Chandler would knock on some attractive neighbors' door. Joey and Chandler would be enticed by the radiantly beautiful women but would carry on with their search. The staff was at a loss as to what joke might work best there.

Astrof, half-conscious, muttered something to himself, and Adam Chase, hearing his comment, quieted the room: "Wait. What did you just say? Say that again." Astrof repeated his suggested line for Joey: "We promised we'd find this monkey. If you see him, he's about yea high, and answers to the name Marcel, so if we could get some pictures of you,

you'd really be helping us out." It was a left-field joke, only made possible by a room too tired, at three or four A.M., to deliver the more obvious punch lines.

Kauffman and Crane were willing to trust their writers' enthusiasm, even when they didn't entirely share it. They would rarely simply veto a story line, preferring to push back against their writers when they felt a pitch was too juvenile or emotionally barren. Greg Malins's pitch about an obstetrician who would enter the room offering an array of facts about Fonzie from *Happy Days* while delivering Phoebe's triplets so thoroughly amused the writers that it made the final version of "The One Hundredth." Crane insisted that the idea made no sense at all, but he was willing to be won over by his writers' enthusiasm.

At other times, the writers could not overcome Kauffman and Crane's skepticism, as with their suggestion for a story line in which Phoebe's gusto for Chinese food leads her to attempt to marry it. "I just find myself not caring," Kauffman would regularly respond to pitches that she felt lacked an emotional through-line. Writer Andrew Reich, trained to write jokes, found it enormously beneficial to have Kauffman and Crane ask questions like "What does Rachel want in this scene?" On occasion, the actors would nix plotlines they could not stomach, as with a story in which Chandler would sneak into a gay bar because he loved the chef's tuna melts. Matthew Perry said no, and the story was shelved.

The atmosphere in the room called for quick wits and a hunger to leap on any opening with the biggest possible joke. Sikowitz remembered one moment in the first season when the writers were approaching a wide-open setup and pondering their choices. In "The One with All the Poker," Rachel was going to enter the room bubbling with excitement, saying, "Guess what, guess what, guess what!" It was an ideal opportunity for a Chandler witticism, but what might he say?

Quicker than Sikowitz could even form a cogent thought, Jeff Astrof burst out with a line: "The fifth dentist caved, and now they're all recommending Trident?" Sikowitz was stunned. Had Astrof known somehow?

Had he prepared the joke in advance? It was a *huge* joke, guaranteed to get an audience response, and Sikowitz had been nowhere near coming up with anything, let alone something as good as that line. It was maddening to be surrounded with people who were that good at being funny.

Sikowitz had his moment later in the process of writing "Poker," when a similar opening announced itself. "Could you *want* her more?" Chandler asks Ross at Central Perk, gesturing offscreen with a rolled-up newspaper. Ross, feigning ignorance, asks, "Who?" Sikowitz leapt in and suggested a line for Chandler: "Dee, the sarcastic sister from *What's Happening!!*" Sikowitz was terribly pleased to have buzzed first on that answer.

For Sikowitz, there was simply nothing better than the sensation of Matt LeBlanc coming over and asking of a particular joke, "Whose was that?" and being able to take the credit. LeBlanc would call them "bombs," meaning a joke that had knocked an audience flat with laughter. He and Matthew Perry in particular hungered for bombs and were intensely pleased when a script gave them an opportunity to dazzle an audience.

Crane and Kauffman had recruited a staff that cared deeply about their characters and took passionate stands about what might have appeared, to less zealous outsiders, as fleeting details. When, early in the first season, the character of Paolo, the hunky Italian lover Rachel meets in "The One with the Blackout," was initially proposed, writer Jeff Greenstein balked. The Latin lover was a tired trope, he insisted, and the show should avoid such lazy, secondhand characters. The room was tied up for most of a day debating how to find a less obvious boyfriend for Rachel to serve as an impediment to her getting together with Ross. For a time, there was serious discussion of transforming Paolo into an Inuit visitor to New York, but the prospect of a stud in mukluks was ultimately deemed to be a bridge too far for audiences.

Jeff Strauss believed that Crane thought of the writers' room as an expansion of his brain. This was not to say that Crane was anxious to take credit for anyone else's work, but rather that, when the room was working in the fashion it was supposed to, Crane would turn to the writers to ably and rapidly flesh out every emotional, uproarious, tender, or bawdy idea he might have, or wish he had.

Crane and Kauffman were gentle and encouraging of their writers, who saw them as figures they wanted to please, and occasionally rebel against. They were ill inclined to crack the whip or insist on getting back to work. They were also perfectionists. Every line had to be the absolute best it could possibly be. Every plot had to be ironclad.

The writers liked to pretend that Crane, who had been born in 1957, had actually come of age in the 1950s, and they poked fun at what seemed to them to be his advanced age (he was thirty-seven when *Friends* premiered) by breaking into the dramatic "DUH-duh-duh" opening of the jazz classic "Sing, Sing, Sing" or fondly reminiscing about that time they had all thought Thomas Dewey was going to be elected president. Crane was like their good-natured dad, willing to withstand the constant ribbing since it emerged from a place of love, even though in some cases he was only a few years older than the writers on his staff.

The writing process was intensely collaborative. Writers might be assigned to craft a first draft of a given script, but by Adam Chase's estimation, 98 percent of the work was actually done in the room. Often, an idea would be filtered through numerous writers, who would add their own flourishes. During the second season, conversation turned to Phoebe while they were writing the episode "The One with the Baby on the Bus." Chase suggested Phoebe play a song called "Smelly Cat." David Crane began to sing the title, and Jeff Astrof chimed in with the line "What are they feeding you?" Someone else contributed the kicker "It's not your fault," and the pillars of "Smelly Cat," which would be Phoebe's most fondly remembered song, had been rapidly assembled.

And the writing staff felt a distinct, and at times surprisingly intense, sense of ownership over their work. During the filming of "The One with the Baby on the Bus," Chase was watching Lisa Kudrow perform "Smelly Cat" and growing increasingly distressed. Kudrow was as funny as ever, but when she reached the chorus, Kudrow was hitting the second word: "Smelly *cat*, smelly *cat*, what are they feeding you?" Chase was insistent that emphasizing *smelly* would be notably funnier and pulled David Crane aside to share his concerns: "I think it's funnier if she hits the first word." Crane was nonplussed: "You seriously want me to go out between takes, in front of a studio audience, and give her that note?"

Chase panicked—what happened to no-name writers who gave acting notes to the stars of their shows?—but held firm. Crane was always willing to go out on a ledge for his writers and gamely stepped onstage to share Chase's suggestion with Kudrow. The scene was, by collective agreement, funnier after Kudrow began emphasizing *smelly* instead of *cat*. But Crane approached Chase after the shoot and told him, "Look, you've got to pick your moments. Because sometimes you're right, but a lot of the time, it's not worth it. If it's three percent funnier, it's not worth it. This time, I'll give it to you."

The writers and cast were working in tandem, and their devotion to delivering the best version of that joke was a notable part of their shared effort. Chase was still early enough in his career that he was fixated on the precise words of the script. What he had written, he thought, was the best possible version of a joke, and it would be a shameful mistake to shoot it any other way but the one the writers had come up with.

The room was like a vampire, forever hungering for fresh blood to suck. And the writers themselves were often content to bite off hunks of their own flesh and transform it into fodder for their characters. The *Friends* characters were the writers' stand-ins and doppelgängers, their adventures and discoveries simultaneously reflections of the writers' own lives and romanticized versions of their more humdrum existences. There was something simultaneously terrifying and cathartic, as Jeff Strauss saw it, about this filtered version of the writers' own reality being passed along to the characters and dispatched to the audience through their television screens.

The trick was not only to mine your own life, but to know which parts were serviceable for the show, which characters might be best served with the autobiographical morsel, and how a funny anecdote might be extended, exaggerated, or adjusted.

Adam Chase had once been in an upscale clothing store with a female friend who suggested a pair of expensive leather pants. Wanting to impress her, he tried them on, and then was swayed by the blandishments of the beautiful store clerk, who told him the pants looked great on him. Six hundred dollars later, Chase owned a pair of pants he would likely never wear again.

The incident was a terrific start but needed more to serve *Friends'* needs. The writers went to work and began to think about what might happen if someone were not only to purchase the leather pants but get stuck in them. The memorable plotline of "The One with All the Resolutions," in which Ross uses a variety of bathroom products in a fruitless attempt to wiggle out of his uncomfortably tight pants ("The lotion and the powder have made a *paste!*") was born.

Stories could come from anywhere. Ted Cohen had once entered a steam room at the gym with his glasses on and had accidentally sat on a fellow patron's knee, inspiring Chandler's sitting on his father-in-law's lap in the sauna in "The One with Phoebe's Cookies." Andrew Reich remembered visiting a friend named Katie who lived in a walk-up apartment with a very narrow staircase. When he got up to Katie's apartment, he noticed she had an oversize couch and wondered just how she had managed to get it up those stairs. Reich brought this thoroughly unremarkable observation back to the room, where it eventually mutated into the memorable "Pivot!" couch-moving sequence from "The One with the Cop."

Comedy writers had a relationship to the world that differed notably from that of civilians. Where the average person sought to bury moments of profound embarrassment or failure, a comedy writer might look at the most humbling or humiliating moments as potential material. One day early in the show's run, Adam Chase was playing with Marta Kauffman's son, Sam, then a toddler, who was visiting the set. He was picking up Sam, tossing him in the air, and then catching him. On about the third attempt, Chase sent Sam hurtling directly into a metal door frame.

Chase saw his career flash before his eyes, convinced that he would be instantly fired from his job for endangering the life of his boss's son. Sam ran off to find his mother, crying hysterically, and Chase went with him, seeking to apologize to Kauffman. She comforted her son but was otherwise unruffled: "I drop him on his head all the time." The incident would eventually serve the third-season episode "The One with the Giant Poking Device," in which Monica accidentally hits Ben's head against a wooden pillar, and he proceeds to dub her "Monica Bang."

And when there was nothing left to mine in your own life, it was time to move on to your friends' shenanigans. Greg Malins remembered hearing about the time when his friend Sebastian Jones had just moved to Los Angeles, carrying a plastic bag filled with his clothing to their mutual friend Brian Boyle's apartment. One day, when Jones was out, Boyle emptied the bag on the floor and proceeded to don every item of Jones's clothing. When Jones came back home, Boyle gestured to himself and said, "Look, I'm wearing all your clothes."

Boyle's prank became Joey's revenge in "The One Where No One's Ready," refitted with a far superior punch line: "Look at me, I'm Chandler. Could I *be* wearing any more clothes?" (Adding to the air of self-referentiality, both Jones and Boyle would join the *Friends* writing staff in later seasons.) Neither Crane nor Kauffman was familiar with the term *going commando,* but when the entire staff urged them to include it, asserting that their audience would instantly understand the reference, they acceded. (Eventually, the *Oxford English Dictionary* would credit *Friends* with one of the earliest recorded usages of the term.)

The squabbles and absurdities of the writers' room found their way into scripts as well. On one occasion, a late-night session was interrupted by someone from the show's office, who poked their head in to tell Greg Malins his fiancée was on the phone. After Malins left the room, writer Michael Borkow said, "Huh. *Wapah!*" All the other writers turned to Borkow, confused. He responded, "You know. He's running out to take a phone call. He's whipped. *Wapah!*" The joke was less about Malins's being "whipped" than a kind of meta-joke about the Stockholm syndrome of the room, in which even taking a phone call felt like a major retreat from commitment. What was funny, though, was the sound that came out of Borkow's mouth.

Chase responded, "That's not the whip sound. This is the whip sound," doing a more traditional "hoo-*pssshh*" crack of the whip. Borkow agreed: "That's what I just did. '*Wapah!*'" Borkow's inability to make a convincing whip-cracking noise became Chandler's struggle in the fourth season's "The One with All the Wedding Dresses."

Kauffman notwithstanding, the *Friends* writers' room was, at the outset, an exceedingly male place, its tastes and interests formed by the concerns of funny young men. (In later years, the staff would have a more even gender balance.) It was left to the few women in the room to push back against plotlines that dismayed them, but while Crane and Kauffman made space for their concerns, this, too, came with a cost.

In the second season, when preparations were commencing for the high-pressure Super Bowl episode, writer Alexa Junge, at the time one of only two female writers on the staff other than Kauffman, took umbrage at what she perceived to be the hackneyed and sexist plotline that pitted Monica and Rachel against each other in competition for movie star Jean-Claude Van Damme. "You know," she told the other writers, "if they're friends they're not going to do that. That's bad for the sisterhood. We would never do that."

Junge was disturbed by the girl-fight vibe of the episode, complete with the wardrobe choices. Why were Monica and Rachel wearing flimsy T-shirts on a cold set on what was supposed to be a winter day, their nipples instantly visible beneath their clothing?

Junge's feminist feathers were ruffled, and she told Crane that she thought the plotline was beneath the show's lofty standards. Crane heard her out and told her, "Listen, I don't exactly understand what some of the politics you're saying are and I get that you're really riled up about it and we actually are going to do this story, but over the course of the day, could you just stop me when something's offensive to you?" Junge felt like she had been put in a difficult position, hired against her will to serve as feminist scold and designated spoilsport, but she dutifully communicated her concerns to Crane over the course of the shoot. (The T-shirts stayed.)

Much of the writing staff was locked in on crafting killer jokes, but to serve in Marta Kauffman and David Crane's writers' room was to receive an ongoing lesson in the balance between comedy and drama. Huge jokes were the white whale they were all hunting, but the romantic through-line that gave episodes like "The One with All the Poker" their meaning clarified that all the jokes in the world could never convince an audience to care about the show's characters.

Kauffman and Crane were permanent reminders in the writers' room that as much as this crew of mostly single, mostly twentysomething smart alecks might have been allergic to sentiment, it was that very sentiment that would win audiences over to *Friends'* side. The room generally agreed that, along with Crane, Kauffman and Junge were among the best at providing the emotional nuances the show needed. Without Ross and Rachel, and the audience's desire to see their relationship through, viewers would never have bothered with the show, no matter how many bombs Chandler or Joey might have dropped.

This was television on the *Cheers* model: joke, joke, joke, joke, until suddenly the ground falls away and a moment of unexpected sentiment retroactively justifies and enriches all the effortless humor that preceded it. Kauffman and Crane's script craft doubled as a series of lessons in humanity, offered free of charge to their youthful staff. For Sikowitz, moments like Ross's tossing a poker game to give Rachel a much-needed victory in "The One with All the Poker" would catch in his throat unexpectedly, and he would find himself saying, "Oh wow—that was cool."

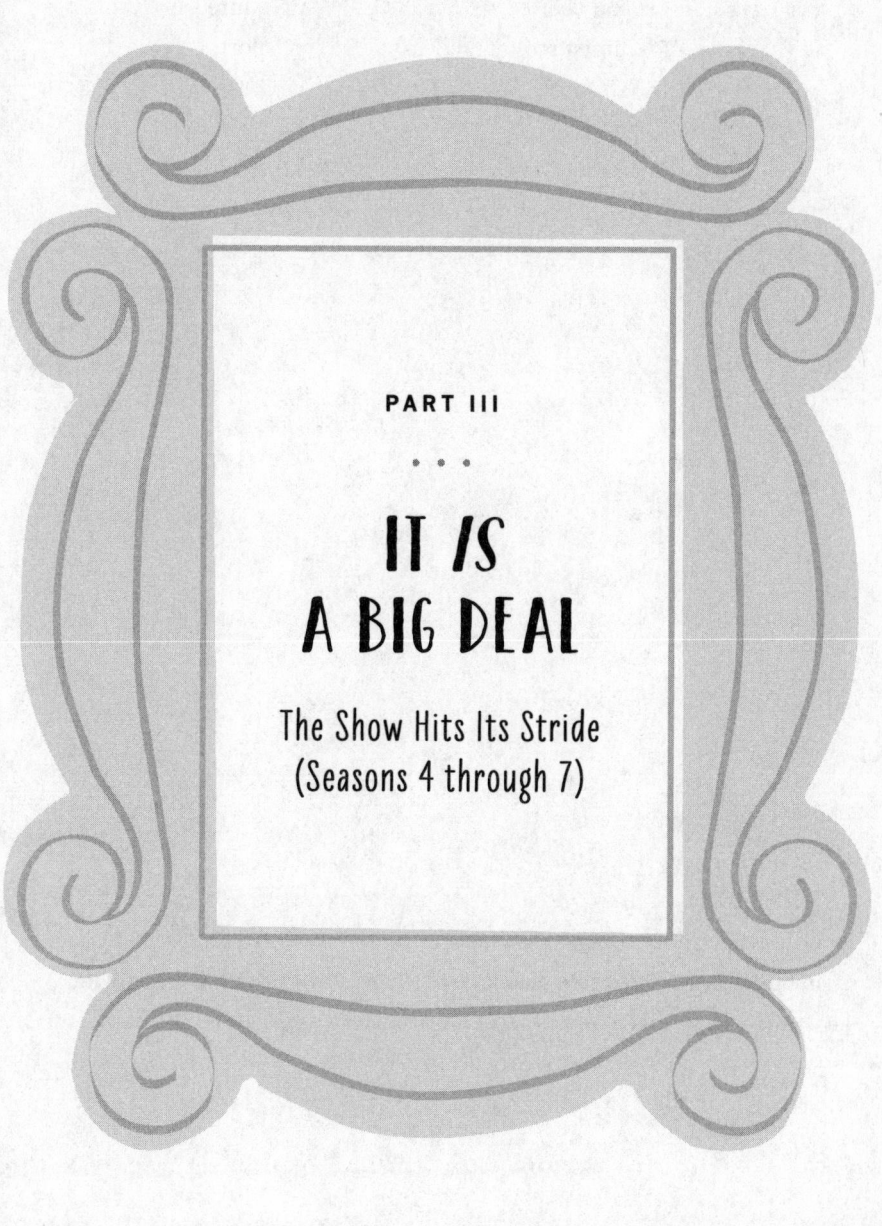

PART III

. . .

IT *IS* A BIG DEAL

The Show Hits Its Stride
(Seasons 4 through 7)

CHAPTER 12

LIGHTNING ROUND

A Look at the Making of an Exemplary Episode

In 2009, when *TV Guide* named the one hundred greatest television episodes of all time, it settled on a single *Friends* episode to inhabit the twenty-first slot: "The One with the Embryos," from the show's fourth season. Fanatics might differ about which *Friends* episode reigns as the series' all-time best—others might vouch for "The One with the Prom Video" or "The One with All the Poker"—but in its belly laughs and its bursts of emotion, in its skillful intermingling of divergent plotlines, and in its surprise denouement, "The One with the Embryos" serves as a template for all that *Friends* did best.

Producing a television show sometimes required adjusting to real-world circumstances. *Friends*' characters were played by actors who lived lives off the set that had to be accommodated, hidden, or transformed. When it came to the fourth season of *Friends*, the tricky encumbrance that the show's writers had to somehow wrestle with was that Lisa Kudrow was pregnant. Some shows had attempted to cover up their star's real-life pregnancy with loose clothing and a sudden interest in carrying around bowling balls and dictionaries (as *Friends* itself would do, after a fashion, with Courteney Cox in its tenth season). Others chose to make their characters pregnant as well.

Kudrow's pregnancy was an opportunity, and a dare. Phoebe was by far the most outrageous of the *Friends* characters and invited the possibility of more unusual circumstances than other characters could have. Phoebe had already discovered a thumb in her can of soda, demonstrated her skepticism about the theory of evolution to Ross, and once whistled at a man and accidentally sent him into a coma. She had been temporarily haunted by the soul of an elderly Jewish woman named Mrs. Adelman.

Phoebe was the receptacle for many of *Friends'* quirkiest impulses, extending the range of the show's comic abilities. She was gleefully, willfully obtuse at times, quizzing Pretenders lead singer Chrissie Hynde about her knowledge of chords or stalking her stalker. She was also demonstrably kind in a fashion not regularly granted to the other characters, giving a homeless woman $1,000 and gently informing Rachel that her boyfriend Paolo had made a pass at her.

The writers often enjoyed writing for Phoebe most, as she required the least tethering to demonstrable reality. Kudrow's daffy sensibility made it seem as if she were laughing at a joke that only she had heard. She appeared to exist on a notably different frequency than her friends, one that the writers frequently turned to as a counterpoint to the more emotionally nuanced existences of the other characters. By the fourth season, Phoebe was past due for her own emotional plotline.

Early in the season, writers began batting around ideas, and the suggestion bubbled up that Phoebe might serve as a surrogate for her brother, Frank Jr. (Giovanni Ribisi, who had also starred in Crane and Kauffman's *Family Album*), and his middle-aged wife, Alice (Debra Jo Rupp). But might Phoebe have more than one baby? Could she have twins? Could she have quintuplets?

Some writers were arguing that Phoebe could have eight babies and that an instant brood in her belly might make for a hilariously over-the-top plotline. Others insisted that eight was far too many and that the story needed to be tempered so as to avoid being too physically dangerous or too unbelievable. They eventually settled on three as the right number—ludicrous enough to be funny but not stretching the bounds of credulity.

Writer Jill Condon was in the shower one morning, pondering the story, when she had a brainstorm: Phoebe should talk to the embryos. She should hold the petri dish with the embryos and implore them to hold on for her brother and sister-in-law's sake. There was never any guarantee, on a show as team-written as *Friends,* that any idea would make it into the script, but as soon as Condon thought of it, she was confident that, unless she was wildly wrong, this moment was likely to make it onto television. It was just what the episode needed. Sure enough, when Condon pitched the idea to the room, David Crane responded enthusiastically: "Let's definitely put that in."

The sentiment in the writers' room was that so overtly sentimental a story needed a more straightforward, comedic B-plot. Seth Kurland emerged with the idea of pitting the remaining characters against each other in a trivia contest, inspired by some screenwriter friends, including future *Kiss Kiss Bang Bang* director Shane Black, who had held a similar competition, which they called the Pad O' Jeopardy, in their apartment, dubbed the Pad O' Guys. Given how extensively the *Friends* characters were invested in each other's lives, wouldn't it be funny to see what they did and did not know about each other?

The writers determined that it would work best as a male vs. female competition, with each team trying to stump the other with the hardest questions they could come up with about their friends. But what could they bet that would provide significant enough stakes to care about? Someone proposed Monica and Rachel betting their apartment on the outcome of the contest, and a quiet moan rippled through the room. This was a flagrant instance of "schmuck bait" storytelling at its most obvious.

"Schmuck bait" was something that tempted the more gullible members of the audience with the promise of enormous changes that more discerning watchers would instantly realize could never actually happen. Schmuck-bait storytelling was a prime example of the kind of lazy, clichéd, corner-cutting work *Friends* eschewed. The writers agreed that they were all better than that.

Then David Crane piped up: "Let's just keep the guys in the girls' apartment." And what had been a tremor of dissatisfaction over bland writing transformed into excitement over a genuine surprise in the works. Condon believed that one of the greatest pleasures television could deliver was a plot development that viewers did not see coming. Very early in the process of writing "The One with the Embryos" (which Crane would later wish he had called "The One with the Contest"), almost the entire writing staff got caught up in the joy of planning a well-executed twist. The girls were going to lose their apartment. Marta Kauffman never bought it, arguing that it stretched the bounds of credulity, but allowed everyone to carry on nonetheless.

"The One with the Embryos" wound up being one of the fastest *Friends* episodes to come together, and, according to Andrew Reich, one of the most enjoyable. "Embryos" departs from *Friends* orthodoxy by eschewing the traditional A-B-C story split; this episode has no C plotline, toggling between only two stories. After a late-night disruption courtesy of Joey and Chandler's chick ("The vet seems to think that she's becoming a rooster. We're getting a second opinion"), the boys gather in Monica and Rachel's apartment the next day and take in the lay of the land.

Joey instantly knows that Monica is wearing her "old-lady underpants" because today is laundry day. Chandler tops him, pointing to Monica and noting that she prefers to eat Tic Tacs in even numbers (a habit that actually belonged to Condon's father) and revealing that Rachel's grocery bag contains a half-eaten box of cookies. Chandler bets the girls $10 that he and Joey can guess all five of the other items in Rachel's bag. They easily rattle off the first four (apples, tortilla chips, diet soda, yogurt), then are stymied by the fifth.

Chandler whispers urgently in Joey's ear, who shakes his head fiercely: "No, no—not for like another two weeks." Joey, a savant of women's bodies, finds that his wisdom extends to knowledge of their menstrual cycles, but this wicked joke also reveals something about the intense awareness of each other's lives that is the bread and butter of *Friends*. The secret of *Friends* is that, ultimately, there are no secrets. Everything eventually sees the light, including what day Rachel is due to have her period. They agree to hold a competition, with Ross as host and quizmaster, and $100 now on the line.

In the next scene, Phoebe is in the doctor's office, where she is surprised to discover that she is having five embryos implanted simultaneously. Frank Jr. and Alice are using all their savings on this one round of implantation, and Phoebe realizes the stakes for her brother.

The remaining friends sit around at home with dreamy looks, taking in the idea of Phoebe's carrying a baby, before jumping up excitedly when Ross makes his announcement: "The test is ready." There will be ten questions for each team, broken down into four categories: Fears and Pet Peeves, Ancient History, Literature, and It's All Relative. The early questions are handled with flair. Monica's pet peeve is animals dressed as humans, and Chandler is scared by Michael Flatley. ("His legs flail about as if independent from his body," Chandler moans.)

Ross asks Monica and Rachel what name appears on the address label of Joey and Chandler's *TV Guide*. Rachel leaps up and says it's Chandler's magazine, only to be corrected by Ross. The *TV Guide* is addressed, he tells her, to Chanandler Bong. Monica, intense as ever, turns to Rachel with displeasure: "Rachel, use your head." Chandler gently corrects Ross, telling him that the *TV Guide* is actually addressed to "*Miss* Chanandler Bong."

Phoebe is back with the embryos and greets them politely, waving at their petri dish: "I'm hoping to be your uterus for the next nine months." She decides to give them a pep talk before they are inserted into her: "We're doing this for Frank and Alice, who you know—you've been there! You know, they want you so much, so when you guys get in there, really grab on." It is a surprisingly emotional moment, with Kudrow, dressed in a hospital gown, shot from above to emphasize her heavy eyelids and the creases lining her forehead. There are laughs in this sequence, but we feel Phoebe's emotion here, her desire to come through for her family in a moment of need.

During the writing process for the episode, Condon obsessively labored over Phoebe's speech to the embryos and felt like she never got it quite right. Once she brought her script back to the room, Crane took a look at the speech and, along with Wil Calhoun, one of the few writers with children, began searching for a more emotional tenor. Condon was still worrying over the sequence and approached Crane. Would it be all right, she wondered, if she took another crack at Phoebe's dialogue? It still was not quite the moment she had envisioned in her mind when the initial burst of inspiration had struck in the shower. Crane agreed, and Condon was moved by his remarkable generosity. He was the boss, but he would never be the one to say that once his golden hands had touched a scene, it was perfect. If someone was volunteering to work even harder on a scene to get it right, Crane would gladly accept their labor.

Back in the apartment, after the name of Chandler's father's all-male burlesque show comes up (Viva Las Gaygas), Ross announces, with the appropriate ring of fervor, the commencement of "the Lightning Round." (He has even made small lightning bolts on his notecards.) The intensity has been cranked up a notch, with Monica telling the boys, "You guys are dead. I am so good at lightning rounds." Chandler has been inspired to compete as well and rouses himself from his usual slumber of apathy to form a solid comeback: "I majored in lightning rounds."

"Wanna bet?" Monica asks. "I'm so confused as to what we've been doing so far," Chandler cracks, but Monica has a bigger pot in mind. Ross, playing the unctuous game-show host, if only in his mind, restates every offer and counteroffer in a hushed tone. When Monica suggests that the boys get rid of the rooster if they win, Rachel is intrigued by the stakes: "Ooh, that's interesting." Rachel then proceeds to up the stakes, wanting the duck thrown in as well ("He gets the other one all riled up"). Chandler accepts, suggesting that if he and Joey win, they get Monica and Rachel's apartment. Monica is at her best when she is at her most crazed, and Cox demonstrates the control freak's buried desire to throw caution to the wind. Risk is her drug.

The trivia game demonstrates Ross's sustained attention to the pasts and foibles of his friends that aligns with the show's. *Friends* is a show about loyalty. "The One with the Embryos" is so successful because it is, among other things, a demonstration of that loyalty and that deep knowledge. It was also an opportunity for the audience to insert themselves into the action. The audience was committed to *Friends* like the show's characters were committed to each other, and the characters' impressive familiarity with the mundane details of each other's lives was a symbolic stand-in for the audience's bottomless interest in accruing that same knowledge.

Fans hungered to know as much about *Friends'* characters as they did, and the brief lightning-round peek into the secrets of their lives was profoundly pleasurable not just because it was funny, but because it satiated the audience's cravings. We, too, wanted to know that Rachel claimed her favorite movie was *Dangerous Liaisons* when it was really *Weekend at Bernie's,* or that Monica's nickname had once been Big Fat Goalie, or the precise number of differing categories of towels Monica had. (Joey and Chandler begin listing some of them—Everyday Use, Fancy, Guest, Fancy Guest—before Joey correctly blurts out "eleven.")

Joey and Chandler acquit themselves well, and it is now Rachel and Monica's turn to answer questions. They know that Joey's imaginary friend was Maurice the space cowboy but are unaware that Chandler was nineteen when he first touched a woman's breast. They are en route to victory when Ross stumps them with a hilariously basic question: "What is Chandler Bing's job?" Amy Toomin and Condon's script brilliantly plays off a latent ambiguity in the show, in which we occasionally see Chandler at work but rarely understand what he is actually doing, beyond its being some fatally bland white-collar drudgery. We, too, cannot really say what it is that Chandler does for a living, and the surprise question is a reminder that the show does not care all that much, either.

Rachel and Monica freeze, then clutch at each other. "Oh gosh," Rachel moans, "it has something to do with numbers."

"And processing!" Monica shouts.

"And he carries a briefcase," Rachel unhelpfully adds. Ross jumps in to tell them that they need this answer or they will lose the game.

"It has something to do with—transponding," says Monica, circling her hands around an invisible globe.

"Oh! Oh! Oh!" Rachel leaps and points in Chandler's direction. "He's a transpond—transpondster!"

Aniston's bobble on the final word underscores the ludicrousness of the moment, in which Rachel has convinced herself her friend has a job she struggles to even pronounce. Monica swivels in her direction, stunned and appalled: "That's not even a word!" Ross's game clock lets out a tinny beep, and Monica releases a primal howl of shock and dismay. Meanwhile, Joey and Chandler leap into the air with delight, their impulsive bet paying off in a fashion they could never have conceived of.

Monica is sure she can salvage the situation and offers to go double-or-nothing. Chandler responds with fake politesse, quietly telling her, "I would never bet this apartment. It's too nice." Rachel declares that she refuses to move, and Monica berates her, telling her that their loss is entirely her fault. (Needless to say, Monica could not come up with Chandler's job title, either.) "That is a boys' apartment," Rachel complains about her proposed new home. "It's dirty and it smells!"

For *Friends,* the differing plots were meant to not merely exist in parallel with each other but intersect, and occasionally echo, each other. Phoebe appears in the next scene, lying upside down in one of Monica and Rachel's chairs ("I'm going to let gravity do its job") and strumming a guitar as she sings to the embryos inside her: "Are you in there, little fetus? In nine months will you come greet us? I will buy you some Adidas."

Frank Jr. and Alice come over with a dubious gift of a lollipop and a home-pregnancy test, and Alice, in true teacher fashion, makes a corny joke out of asking if Phoebe is in the mood to take a one-question exam. Phoebe reluctantly agrees, and disappears into the bathroom as the apartment argument flares up once more.

In one of the most iconic moments of *Friends'* ten-year run, destined to be repeated in practically every future montage sequence for the show, Chandler is wheeled in riding Joey's dog sculpture, a slacker monarch wielding a sandwich as his scepter. Jill Condon was fixated on the horrifying ceramic dog that Joey had purchased for his short-lived uptown apartment in "The One Where Eddie Moves In" and that had been rescued by Ross when the repo men had arrived to take it away. It was the ideal symbol of the boys' tacky sensibility and precisely the kind of piece that would upend Monica's tasteful décor. What if Chandler came into his new apartment riding the ceramic dog? Assistant director Ben Weiss placed the dog on a dolly and had it rolled into the apartment.

Writing for television meant imagining words and actions that would be carried out by actors. The results were rarely as viscerally satisfying as the pleasure of solving a narrative problem. But in this case, when Condon stood on the set and watched the door to the apartment open and Matthew Perry fling his arms wide with glee, she felt a rush of satisfaction. This was every bit as good as she had hoped it would be.

"You are mean boys who are just being mean!" Rachel childishly grouses at Chandler's lavish display of triumph. Chandler continues to milk the situation for every ounce of aggravation he can, mock-pleading with everyone: "Would you all stop yelling in our apartment? You are *ruining* moving day for us." That Chandler is eating a sandwich as he speaks undercuts his authority, and also emphasizes the extent to which this entire apartment switch is a marvelous lark for the boys at the same time that it is a life-changing catastrophe for Rachel and Monica.

The shouting is reaching a new crescendo of outrage and displeasure when Phoebe, forgotten already, reemerges from the bathroom with a white stick in hand, anxious to share her news: "You guys, you're going to have a baby. They're going to have a baby!" Frank Jr., clad in an unflattering gray Members Only jacket zipped up to his throat, raises his arms in *Rocky*-esque triumph: "My sister's going to have my baby!" Everyone spontaneously gathers to enfold Phoebe in a group hug.

"The One with the Embryos" craftily alternates between its major and minor plots, between weightless twentysomething antics and significant life changes. Condon and Toomin's script expertly switches between the two, letting us sink into the endlessly charming mire of the apartment competition before yanking the floor out with Phoebe's unexpected announcement.

Friends is charming for its big-picture portrait of how being young and confused and free gradually evolves into being older and wiser and more rooted, but also for its abiding interest in the absurdities of youth. Phoebe's announcement is the emotional high point of "The One with the Embryos," but the episode prefers to end with an image of Joey and Chandler, ensconced in their new apartment, simultaneously leaning back in their painfully ugly, overstuffed leather recliners, releasing twin grunts of pleasure. (The presence of the chairs themselves was inspired by Ira Ungerleider's attempt, once upon a time, to stay in his La-Z-Boy for an entire weekend.) They proceed to lean back even farther, now both practically recumbent and giddy with pleasure. This is their home now.

"Embryos" was a triumph for emphasizing a certain tendency in *Friends'* handling of its characters that had previously gone mostly unmentioned. What prior sitcom had expressed so deep an interest in its protagonists' past lives? Most sitcoms existed in an eternal present, where little change was encouraged or acknowledged, and the past was generally a single, flat narrative arc—Mary Richards moving to Minneapolis, or Gilligan and his friends washing up on a desert island. The idea of mining characters' histories for narrative material was foreign to the sitcom. But from the very outset, *Friends* was telling us about what had already happened to its characters elsewhere.

"The One Where Monica Gets a Roommate"—Rachel (Jennifer Aniston) arrives at Central Perk in her wedding dress in the series' pilot episode, having fled her own wedding.   NBCU Photo Bank © 1994/NBCUniversal/Getty Images

"The One Where Ross and Rachel . . . You Know"—Chandler and Joey's goofy, deeply committed friendship was only enhanced by the arrival of their matching Barcaloungers. Their grunts of satisfaction at fully reclining were the perfect expression of their doofusy delight in small pleasures. *Paul Drinkwater/NBC/NBCU Photo Bank © 1996/NBCUniversal/Getty Images*

"The One Where No One's Ready"—"I'm Chandler. Could I *be* wearing any more clothes?" Joey (Matt LeBlanc) does lunges in front of his roommate, Chandler (Matthew Perry), while clad in the entirety of his wardrobe. NBCU Photo Bank © 1996/NBCUniversal/Getty Images

"The One with the Embryos"—Chandler and Joey celebrate their incredible good fortune at winning the trivia contest and taking possession of Rachel and Monica's apartment. *J. Delvalle © 1998/NBCUniversal/Getty Images*

"The One in Vegas"—Ross (David Schwimmer) pleads for absolution in a Las Vegas hotel room as Rachel (Jennifer Aniston) displays her surprisingly trim goatee, drawn on with a Sharpie as a prank gone terribly wrong. NBC/NBCU Photo Bank © 1999/NBCUniversal/Getty Images

MATTHEW 8/19

SCHWIM 11-2

Polaroids taken on set of the show's stars Matthew Perry, Matt LeBlanc, Jennifer Aniston, and David Schwimmer. (David Crane appears in the background of Aniston's shot.)

Jennifer Aniston and set decorator Greg Grande wielding celebratory cigars on set.